THE TRUTH ABOUT BUYING ANNUITIES

Steve Weisman

Publishing as FT Press
Upper Saddle River, New Jersey 07458

Printed in the United States of America

Second Printing December 2008

ISBN-10: 0-13-235308-3
ISBN-13: 978-0-13-235308-3

Pearson Education LTD.
Pearson Education Australia PTY, Limited.
Pearson Education Singapore, Pte. Ltd.
Pearson Education North Asia, Ltd.
Pearson Education Canada, Ltd.
Pearson Educatión de Mexico, S.A. de C.V.
Pearson Education—Japan
Pearson Education Malaysia, Pte. Ltd.

Library of Congress Cataloging-in-Publication Data

Weisman, Steve.
The truth about buying annuities / Steve Weisman.
p. cm.
ISBN 0-13-235308-3 (pbk. : alk. paper) 1. Annuities. I. Title.
HG8790.W44 2009
368.3'7--dc22

2008005622

Vice President, Publisher
Tim Moore
Associate Publisher and Director of Marketing
Amy Neidlinger
Executive Editor
Jim Boyd
Operations Manager
Gina Kanouse
Development Editor
Russ Hall
Digital Marketing Manager
Julie Phifer
Publicity Manager
Laura Czaja
Assistant Marketing Manager
Megan Colvin
Marketing Assistant
Brandon Smith
Cover and Interior Designs
Stuart Jackman, Dorling Kindersley
Managing Editor
Kristy Hart
Senior Project Editor
Lori Lyons
Copy Editor
Water Crest Publishing, Inc.
Design Manager
Sandra Schroeder
Senior Compositor
Gloria Schurick
Manufacturing Buyer
Dan Uhrig

To Carole, who makes all my ordinary days extraordinary. The dividends on our investment in a marriage license continue to outperform any annuity.

Saving for retirement used to be so easy. Companies provided pensions that would pay their retired workers for the rest of their lives, not to mention the fact that companies would also pay for health insurance for retirees. On top of that, there was workers' own savings. And don't forget the Social Security check that came in the mail every month. Retirees were set for the rest of their lives.

But times have changed. People are living longer. Baby Boomers facing retirement can expect to live considerably longer, but not necessarily healthier, lives than their parents. They will spend much more time in retirement. But few companies offer the kind of guaranteed, defined-benefit pension plan that formerly was so common. The 401(k) is king, and although it provides the potential for considerable retirement savings, it takes some effort and commitment by workers today to provide for tomorrow. As for health insurance, all too often companies are telling retirees that they are on their own. In addition, people are not saving as much as they did in the past. And even that Social Security check doesn't seem quite as secure as it once did.

Things look rough for retirees.

But to the rescue have come insurance companies and others with a product that guarantees it will provide retirement income for the rest of your life. The product is the annuity. It is not a new idea, but it may be an idea whose time has come, with close to 2 trillion dollars now invested in all kinds of annuities.

But is this the answer to our problems?

According to H.L. Mencken, "For every problem, there is a solution that is simple, neat, and wrong." Well, annuities are far from simple. And although they may appear neat, they are quite complicated. They also are dead wrong for many people who own them, particularly elderly purchasers of deferred variable annuities, who were sold inappropriate annuities by salespeople more interested in the high commissions that annuities bring to salespeople than in helping their clients.

But are annuities always wrong?

The answer is no. Annuities have much not to like about them, including high fees along with misleading and sometimes illusory benefits. However, this investment, which has been around since early Roman times, has evolved and continues to evolve in an effort by insurance companies and other legitimate issuers of annuities to provide secure retirement income for people. If you look hard enough, you can find lower fee annuities that provide benefits which may be tailored to your particular retirement needs.

But you need to know the truth.

Perhaps nowhere in the investment world is there more misleading and downright wrong information about an investment product than with annuities. But this book will tell you the truth. It explains, in clear and understandable language, basic information you need to know about the many different types of annuities. It tells you what the pitfalls of annuities are. It tells you about the lies and misrepresentations to avoid. It also tells you about where annuities might play a useful part in your own retirement planning, when to use them, and how to use them.

It gives you the rules in simple and concise language so that armed with this information, you can make an intelligent and confident decision as to whether annuities should be a part of your retirement planning. Oscar Wilde said, "A man who does not think for himself, does not think at all." This book will give you the knowledge you need to make an informed decision for yourself about one of the most important issues you will face for the rest of your life—how to make your money last a lifetime.

TRUTH 1

The history of annuities

"I advise you to go on living solely to enrage those who are paying your annuities. It is the only pleasure I have left."

—Voltaire

Annuities have had a rich and colorful history. The early Romans, inventors of such innovations as the public bath, the iron padlock, and the calendar, also developed the first annuities. In fact, the term "annuities" may have come from the Latin term "annua," which means "annual stipend." In ancient Rome, people would make a single payment in return for annual lifetime payments. Even then, retirement planning was a concern. Roman jurist Domitius Ulpianus developed the first known mortality table used for annuity purposes. Although he had little in the way of data, his actuary tables were found to be effective and were used for more than a thousand years.

Early annuities also were used by governments to raise money to fight the many wars deemed necessary by the rulers of seventeenth century Europe. Even in the middle ages, increased taxes were not a particularly popular activity for the populace. Into this environment, a particularly intriguing form of annuity came into being, known as the "tontine." Under the direction of French King Louis XIV, to find a non-taxing way to fund ongoing wars, Minister of Finance Cardinal Mazarin hired Lorenzo Tonti, an Italian banker. Tonti developed the tontine in 1652. In 1693, the government of the United Kingdom established a state-sponsored tontine. Under the terms of a tontine, participants would purchase shares in the tontine. In return, they received income for life. The most interesting aspect of the tontine was that as more and more participants died, the annuity payments to surviving participants increased substantially until the final surviving tontine participant received a huge lottery-like payment. This one financial product combined, in effect, a war tax, a lifetime payment plan, and a lottery. Life in the middle ages did not get much better than that. The popularity of the tontine even extended to early America, where in 1790, Alexander Hamilton developed a form of tontine to reduce national debt. Unfortunately, the greatest lure to investors of the tontine—the possibility of a lottery-like windfall to the final participant—also was its downfall, as the inducement to hasten the death of other participants was deemed too much of an encouragement to murder. By the 1900s, tontines were gone from the annuity world.

Annuities were often used during the 1700s by European countries to raise money instead of either taxing or offering bonds, such as is done today. Initially these annuities were sold to everyone at the same price without any consideration of the age or sex of the annuity purchaser. Over time, as actuarial patterns were observed, the cost of annuities became more refined.

The greatest lure to investors of the tontine—the possibility of a lottery-like windfall to the final participant—also was its downfall, as the inducement to hasten the death of the other participants was deemed too much of an encouragement to murder.

Annuities first appeared in America in 1759 when Pennsylvanian Presbyterian ministers were able to purchase lifetime annuity contracts from the Corporation for the Relief of Poor and Distressed Presbyterian Ministers and Distressed Widows and Children of Ministers, a company whose existence lasted almost as long as its name. However, the general public was not particularly attracted to annuities as a vehicle for retirement planning because, at that time, the best retirement planning was to have a large family that would take care of you in what passed for old age during America's early years. The first annuities available to the general public were not sold in America until 1912; however, the popularity of annuities did not take off until the Great Depression. Concerns as to the risks inherent in investing in the stock market motivated more and more people to buy annuities from large, stable insurance companies to pay for their retirement. These publicly available annuities were pretty basic in format. Unlike the stock market, the annuities guaranteed the return of your principal, as well as income at a fixed rate. Payments from the annuities could either be taken over a specific period of years or a fixed income for life. Legislation enabling the general availability of annuities was enacted in the 1930s shortly after the enactment of Social Security. At the time, Social Security was not intended to provide the primary funds for the retirement needs of aging Americans. Rather, it was intended to merely supplement retirement planning that would be done by individuals themselves through such investment vehicles as annuities. The tax deferral aspect of annuities was made a part of the early annuity laws to further encourage people to provide for their own retirement.

Variable annuities made their appearance on the annuity landscape in 1952, when some creative actuaries came up with the first annuities that would base their payout upon the performance of separate investment accounts held within the annuity. The Teachers Insurance and Annuities Association–College Retirement Equity Fund, commonly referred to as TIAA-CREF, sold the first variable annuities. Early variable annuity purchasers were able to choose from a limited number of investment accounts to have as the basis for their annuities. However, due to regulatory complexities, the major insurance companies did not generally sell variable annuities until 1960; it was not until the passage of the Tax Equity and Fiscal Responsibility Act (TEFRA) in 1982 that the modern variable annuity was born. Over the years, legislation has continued to appear from time to time to curb practices considered abusive—as in 1988, when the Tax and Miscellaneous Revenue Act (TAMRA) was enacted to tighten loopholes created by the earlier Tax Reform Act of 1986.

Today's annuities... offer many more choices to investors to tailor their annuities to their own specific needs and desires.

Today's annuities may not be as much fun as the tontine of the 1700s, but they offer many more choices to investors to tailor their annuities to their own specific needs and desires. Greater expansion of investment choices to individuals within their variable annuities, death benefits (an oxymoron, if ever there was one), and reduced surrender charges are all developments that are a part of the evolution of the annuity.

TRUTH 2

Immediate annuities

“The question isn’t at what age I want to retire, it’s at what income.”

—George Foreman

Immediate annuities are a financial product designed to provide you with an income stream for life. They are bought with a single lump-sum payment and begin to make payments to you right away. Instant gratification. What could be more American than that? For example, you give the insurance company, say, $100,000, and it pays you $600 per month for the rest of your life. Immediate annuities can either be fixed rate or variable rate.

Fixed rate annuities

The fixed immediate annuity pays regular payments at a specific locked-in interest rate on either a monthly, quarterly, semi-annual, or annual basis. Each payment consists of a partial return of your initial investment along with earnings. The amount of the monthly payment depends on your age and the options that you chose within the annuity contract. An immediate annuity can provide you with income for life or even for the lifetime of you and your spouse. Alternatively, it can be structured to provide income for periods of up to 20 years. The amount of your monthly payment that relates to the money you initially put into the annuity is tax-free. However, the earnings portion of your monthly payment is subject to income tax. Fixed immediate annuities are a good investment for older people who are afraid of outliving their savings. They also are attractive to people who either don't understand the stock market or believe they do understand it and find it too unpredictable a place to invest for their retirement.

Fixed immediate annuities are a good investment for older people who are afraid of outliving their savings.

A fixed immediate annuity works best for you if you think that you will live longer than the insurance company actuaries think you will. With life insurance, you win if you die early because you get (or more accurately, your beneficiaries get) a large sum of money after paying a small amount of premium. With lifetime fixed immediate annuities, you win by living longer than the company actuaries predict because you are paid by the company for as long as you live, regardless of how much money you put into the annuity.

The older you are when you purchase a fixed immediate annuity, the more the company issuing the annuity is willing to pay you. This has nothing to do with the company being favorably inclined toward the elderly, but everything to do with their belief that the older you are, the more likely you are to die sooner. And just as people like to hedge their bets at the horse races by betting on more than one horse to win, you can also hedge your bet on your fixed immediate annuity by choosing an option that will require the company to continue to pay your beneficiaries if you die earlier than might be expected. This option to have payments continue even after your death is available for specific periods of time, ranging from five to twenty years. Obviously, however, if you purchase such an option, your cost will be greater and your payout less than if you just rolled the dice and bought a fixed immediate annuity that provided for payments only during your lifetime, because the company is bound to pay for a longer period of time. A similar, but less costly, alternative is to buy an annuity that will pay to your beneficiary the balance of whatever you initially paid for the annuity if you die before having at least received back what you initially paid the company.

Variable immediate annuities

Unlike the fixed immediate annuity, the amount you receive through a variable immediate annuity changes depending upon the return on the portfolio of investments that form the basis of your annuity. Unlike the fixed immediate annuity, the amount that you receive monthly is never guaranteed at any set amount. For many people who choose annuities in order to avoid the confusing array of investment choices available to them outside of annuities, having to choose the underlying investments in their annuities tends to compound the confusion of an investment that is confusing enough on its own.

The amount you receive through a variable immediate annuity changes depending upon the return on the portfolio of investments that form the basis of your annuity.

The choices within a variable annuity are usually limited to an array of investments similar to mutual funds, called *sub-accounts*. The sub-accounts, in turn, may be composed exclusively of stocks, bonds, money market instruments, or a mixture of these investments. These sub-accounts may appear to be the same as mutual funds offered by the same investment managers to the general public as stand-alone mutual funds, but they are prohibited by law from being the exact same mutual funds. The return of investment on these sub-accounts can differ significantly from a mutual fund offered to the public by the same mutual fund manager.

TRUTH 3

Fixed rates

"An investment in knowledge always pays the best interest."

—Benjamin Franklin

If your dog or cat could talk, they probably would tell you that they are not too thrilled about being "fixed." But when it comes to a guaranteed fixed rate on their annuities, owners are pretty happy with the security of knowing that the rate of return they will be receiving from their annuity is fixed. People equate a fixed rate with a safe and secure investment. But fixed has a different meaning to the insurance companies issuing the fixed rate annuity than it may to you.

Insurance companies go by their version of the Golden Rule, which is that since they have the gold, they get to make the rules. And, according to their rules, the fixed interest rate that they promise to pay you on your annuity is not necessarily fixed for the full term of your annuity, but rather only for whatever period they decide they will guarantee a specific fixed rate.

Buried within the fine print of your fixed rate annuity may be a provision stating that the guaranteed fixed rate you are credited with in your annuity is guaranteed only for as little as a year; if you shop around, however, you can find companies that will guarantee their interest rate for as long as ten years. The actual interest rate you receive after the guarantee period is determined by the insurance company. Although there is indeed a minimum guaranteed rate, that rate is low—generally around 3%. For example, although the rate that attracted you to the particular annuity is guaranteed for only one year, you are left with a surrender period that will penalize you if you decide to leave the annuity for a better-paying investment at the end of that first year.

Buried within the fine print of your fixed rate annuity may be a provision that states that the guaranteed fixed rate that you are credited with in your annuity is only guaranteed for as little as a year.

Generally, as with Certificates of Deposit, the longer the length of the duration of the annuity, the higher the interest rate that the insurance company will commit to. In fact, you may find a close correlation between the guaranteed rates in a fixed rate annuity and the rates for a bank-issued Certificate of Deposit for a similar period.

I don't know the investment track record of Nostradamus, but when you are trying to determine whether you are better served by a long- or short-term annuity, a key factor is whether you think interest rates will rise or fall in the upcoming years. If you think interest rates will be rising, you will want to commit to the shortest period possible so that at the end of your annuity, you can get a new annuity with a new, higher interest rate. On the other hand, if you think that interest rates are likely to go down, you will want to get an annuity with the longest period of a guaranteed interest rate.

Look for annuities that guarantee your rate for the longest period possible.

TIP Look for annuities that guarantee your rate for the longest period possible. Some companies will guarantee your rate for as long as ten years. Also look for an annuity that does not have a surrender period that lasts longer than the guaranteed interest period, so if it makes sense for you to get out of the annuity, you can do so without having to pay a surrender fee. This is particularly important because once your initial guarantee period has run out, you are like Blanche DuBois in *A Streetcar Named Desire*, depending on the kindness of strangers—in this case, the strangers at the insurance company to determine the return on your investment. You also should ask your annuity salesperson for documentation of the renewal rate history of the company offering an annuity you are considering buying. If the company you are considering has a history of paying competitive rates even after the guarantee periods have lapsed, you can certainly feel more comfortable dealing with them.

TIP If you presently have an annuity that is beyond the initial guaranteed interest period, yet still within the surrender period, you are not entirely without options. You can make a tax-free 1035 exchange and purchase a more appropriate annuity that will pay you a higher interest rate for a longer period. (You can learn more about 1035 exchanges in Truth 19, "Tax-Free 1035 Exchanges.") Of course, if you are still within the surrender period of your original annuity, you will have to do a bit of math to calculate how much more you will earn with the new annuity and how long it will take you to recoup the cost of the surrender fees incurred when you exchange your original annuity for the new annuity. As a matter of investment strategy, also consider the length of the new surrender period, which comes with the new annuity.

Time to bail

An important provision in a fixed rate annuity is the Bail Out provision. This term, which is found within the fine print of your annuity contract, permits you to get out of your annuity without any penalty if, after the initial guaranteed interest rate period, the insurance company renews your annuity at an interest rate that is lower than the original rate by at least an amount designated within your annuity contract, which may be 1%. For example, if you had an initial guaranteed interest rate of 5% and, at the end of your guarantee period, the insurance company offered a new guaranteed rate of 4%, you would have a specific period of time after receiving notice of the proposed renewal rate to decide whether to either accept the new guaranteed rate or take your money out of the annuity without having to pay any surrender fees. It is important to remember, however, that if you do withdraw your money from an annuity to invest in something other than an annuity, you will be subject to a substantial federal income tax penalty if you are under the age of 59½. On the other hand, it should be noted that if you decide not to bail out and instead accept the new guaranteed interest rate, a new surrender charge period also begins.

TRUTH 4

Deferred annuities

"The future ain't what it used to be."

—Yogi Berra

Deferred annuities are annuities you purchase that will not begin to pay you until some time in the future as specified within your annuity, although you can choose to end the deferral period earlier. They may pay you in the future at a fixed rate or a variable rate. The amounts that you receive from a fixed rate deferred annuity can vary considerably from what you may receive from a variable rate deferred annuity.

Deferred annuities are investments that are bought for retirement. For many people, they represent the umbrella to protect themselves from those rainy days that may come after retirement. However, it may not be advantageous to put your money into an investment in which you will have greatly limited access to your money until you are at least 59 ½ years old and have held the investment long enough to free yourself of the surrender fees commonly found in annuities. Fortunately, although it is not easy for you to get at your money during the early years of your annuity, it is also not easy for Uncle Sam to get at your money in the annuity either. Until you withdraw money from your annuity, your earnings grow tax-deferred, which represents the primary advantage of owning an annuity. The longer you keep your money in the annuity, the more it grows without being taxed.

The amounts that you receive from a fixed rate deferred annuity can vary considerably from what you may receive from a variable rate deferred annuity.

The period during which your annuity investment grows untouched by you and the government is called the *accumulation phase*. During this period, you are also covered by the death benefit part of the annuity contract. The terms of the death benefit may vary significantly from policy to policy, but they all share one common characteristic—they vanish once the accumulation phase is over. Once you start to take your money out of the annuity, the death benefit ceases to apply except as an additional costly provision.

Deferred annuities can either be fixed rate or variable rate annuities. A typical fixed rate deferred annuity purchaser is someone who is somewhat risk adverse. As Jerry Seinfeld would say, "Not that there is anything wrong with that." No investment is worthwhile if it keeps you up at night worrying about it. For these people, bank-issued Certificates of Deposit are an investment with which they are comfortable. Forget about the fact that when you factor in inflation, many people who have their investments primarily invested in Certificates of Deposit are merely going broke a bit more slowly; the fact is that they know the rate of return they are going to receive and are comfortable that it is guaranteed by the federal government. With Certificates of Deposit, the longer you are willing to commit your money to the bank, the greater the return the bank is willing to pay. Similarly, the fixed rate deferred annuity, which may be for a period of anywhere from one to five years, also guarantees you a fixed rate of return. As with the bank CD, the longer you commit your money to the company issuing the annuity, generally the greater the fixed rate you will receive. This rate of return does not provide much of a protection from inflation, but that is not the attraction of a fixed rate deferred annuity—the attraction is its safety, security, and guarantee. This time the guarantee is from a particular company issuing the annuity rather than the federal government. Nonetheless, if you carefully research the company from which you are considering buying an annuity, you should be able to sleep well at night.

The attraction [of a fixed rate deferred annuity] is its safety, security, and guarantee.

A variable rate deferred annuity is somewhat of a hybrid between a fixed deferred annuity and a mutual fund. It has a portion of the annuity referred to as the general account that guarantees you a minimum fixed rate of return on your investment for a specific period of time. However, the bulk of the investment portion of your annuity is held in mutual fund–like investments referred to as sub-accounts.

When you reach the end of the deferral period of your deferred annuity, you have some choices to make. One option available to you is to roll over the annuity into another annuity as a tax-free 1035 exchange. If you don't have an immediate need for your money, this

When you reach the end of the deferral period of your deferred annuity, you have some choices to make.

option permits you to continue the tax-deferred growth of your money. However, it is important to note that when you do exchange your old annuity for a new annuity, you start the surrender penalty period again, which becomes a more significant factor as you age.

Another option is to cash in the annuity, pay the taxes on your earnings, and invest the money in another investment appropriate for you at that time. This sounds like a simple thing to do, but it is important to remember that all the earnings of your annuity are subject to income tax at high ordinary income tax rates regardless of the fact that with a variable annuity, the basis for your profits are the performance of mutual fund sub-accounts. If you had held these same funds outside of the annuity, they would have been taxed when cashed in at lower capital gains rates.

A third option is to annuitize the annuity, whereby you spread out the return of your principal and earnings over a period of time. One important fact to remember is that once you have annuitized the contract, you cannot change your mind even if your circumstances change. Fortunately, however, many companies will permit you to make systematic withdrawals without actually annuitizing the contract. The amount of your withdrawals can be made flexible enough to adapt to changes in your needs. Unfortunately, the cost of this flexibility is a greater tax bill from the IRS because all the money you take out of your annuity through a systematic withdrawal is subject to income tax until you have taken out all of your earnings. Alternatively, if you annuitize your annuity, a portion of your regular payments is considered an untaxable return of your principal.

TRUTH 5

Annuity fees

"Beware of little expenses. A small leak will sink a great ship."

—Benjamin Franklin

As with any investment, it is not important what you earn, but rather what you keep. A major concern with annuities as an investment, particularly variable annuities, is the myriad of fees that can eat away at the value of your investment. An unfortunate aspect of annuity fees is that the cost of many of them may not be apparent to you.

Commissions or sales charges

Many annuities trumpet the fact that you may not be required to pay a sales charge when you first buy an annuity. Salespeople will tell you that the insurance company pays them, and that all the money you use to buy the annuity is working right away for your benefit. The truth is that this is hardly accurate. In fact, although the hefty commissions paid to the annuity salesperson—ranging from 4% to 8% of the amount of your investment, or as much as 15% for some Equity Index Annuities—are indeed paid by the insurance company, the cost of this commission is recaptured through a number of fees that you pay regularly to maintain your annuity. It is a matter of common sense that the high commissions paid by the insurance company translate into high fees for you.

As with any investment, it is not important what you earn, but rather what you keep.

Surrender fees

Many annuities carry surrender fees that are worse than those suffered by General Custer. Annuities should always be seen as long-term investments. In order to discourage people from cashing in their variable annuities, they carry surrender charges that can substantially penalize you for as long as ten years if you cash out your annuity. The most common surrender fees are in effect for the first seven years that you own an annuity. It is common to have the fee be as much as 7% of the value of the annuity in the first year and decline by 1% per year for each of the next six years. It is for this reason that variable annuities are not a particularly appropriate investment for older investors who may need to access their money within the surrender periods. This is one of the main reasons that the North American Securities Administrators Association consistently names variable annuities as one of its top ten scams of the year. It is not that variable annuities in and of themselves represent a scam, but the sale of them by unscrupulous salespeople to elderly investors who are not informed of the substantial costs, penalties, and limitations connected with variable annuities make them an unsuitable investment for people who cannot be confident that they will hold their annuities for at least ten years. Generally, however, you are able to withdraw up to 10% of the value of the annuity per year without incurring a surrender fee.

Mortality and expense charges

This fee is generally buried in the fine print. It covers the cost to the insurance company of the life insurance component of the annuity, the commissions paid by the insurance company to salespeople, and their regular administrative costs in regard to the annuity. The cost to you is usually around 1.1% of the value of the annuity. This means that if you had a $100,000 annuity, you would annually be paying $1,100 to cover this fee, which makes it an expensive way to buy life insurance.

Investment management fees

Just as you would pay a management fee to a mutual fund that you owned as a separate investment, in addition to your regular annuity administrative fees, you pay management fees to the managers of the mutual funds that make up the sub-accounts within your annuity. Don't spend a lot of time looking for this fee; it is deducted from your investment returns, along with mortality and expense fees and administrative fees before the reported accumulated unit value (AUV) of the annuity is calculated and provided to you.

Contract maintenance fee

Although some people might find this fee redundant, the insurance company also charges an annual fixed fee of up to $50 for the record keeping and administrative costs involved in maintaining your annuity. You may find that an eager salesperson will brag about the fact that the contract maintenance fee will remain the same low fee throughout the life of the annuity. They are much less apt to brag, however, about the fact that this is more than made up for with the little disclosed (except in the initial, often-hard-to-read prospectus) Mortality and Expense charge that not only is a large fee, but also continually increases as the value of your annuity rises.

The bottom line

The fees and costs of a variable annuity can have a serious effect on how much you ultimately profit from its purchase. An investment of $5,000 in a mutual fund with typical annual expenses of 1.5% that earned the historically conservative return of 8% would provide you with $431,874 after thirty years. An identical investment of $5,000 in a variable annuity with typical annual expenses of 2.5% that earned, through the sub-accounts, the same 8% return would only provide you with $362,177, a difference of $69,697. In addition, when you pay income taxes on the sale of mutual fund shares, you are taxed at a lower capital gains rate; however, when you take income out of your annuity, even though that income is ultimately derived from a mutual fund held in a sub-account of the annuity, you pay income taxes at higher ordinary income rates.

If the fees do not entirely dissuade you from choosing an annuity, it is imperative that you do your homework. Not all annuities are created equal. The truth is that there are tremendous variations in the fees charged by various insurance companies and other companies issuing annuities. Annuities offered by mutual fund companies Vanguard and T. Rowe Price have significantly lower fees in their variable annuities than you will find in annuities offered by most insurance companies. For those of you who are curious as to how a mutual fund company is able to issue a variable annuity with an insurance component, the answer is quite simple—they do so in conjunction with a life insurance company, just as life insurance companies issue annuities with mutual fund components by partnering up with a mutual fund company.

The fees and costs of a variable annuity can have a serious effect on how much you ultimately profit from its purchase.

TRUTH 6

Variable annuities

"The pure and simple truth is rarely pure and never simple."

—Oscar Wilde

The deferred variable annuity is the redheaded stepchild of annuities. Many people, including myself, believe that they are not a suitable investment for most people. They are a perfectly legal product that, when sold to people for whom they are not suited, give annuities and annuity salespeople a bad name. However, for some people, they can be a good investment.

Let's start with the basics. Variable annuities have been described as being mutual funds wrapped in life insurance. To this definition, I would add "and covered with fees," which is one of the major problems with variable annuities. They are just too damn expensive.

Variable annuities have been described as being mutual funds wrapped in life insurance. To this definition, I would add "and covered with fees."

There are three major components to a variable annuity: a general account, sub-accounts, and the death benefit. The *general account* operates like a fixed annuity. In essence, it is the promise of the insurance company to pay you a guaranteed rate of interest on the money in the account for a specific period of time, which may be anywhere from one to five years or more. However, this is not a terribly significant part of a variable annuity because if you wanted a guaranteed interest rate to be provided by your annuity, you would have purchased a fixed annuity. The lion's share of your investment in a variable annuity—and make no mistake about it, this is an investment, not another form of a savings account—goes into sub-accounts. *Sub-accounts* are essentially mutual funds that are managed by mutual fund companies, such as Fidelity and Vanguard (both of which also offer their own low-cost annuities). Although the law prohibits these funds from exactly mirroring the regular mutual funds that they manage outside of an annuity, they are pretty close.

What you get as a return on your investment is tied directly to the performance of the mutual funds that make up the sub-accounts within your annuity. This means that you have the potential for substantial gains or substantial losses. However, one of the surface attractions of variable annuities to risk-adverse investors is the insurance company's guarantee to you that if you die at a time when the value of your annuity is less than what you paid for it, your beneficiaries will receive a *death benefit* that will be equal to your contribution to the annuity (minus any withdrawals from the annuity that you might have made). This may seem somewhat attractive to you because it would appear that your investment is ultimately guaranteed not to lose money, but that guarantee is somewhat misleading. First of all, variable annuities are purchased primarily as a retirement investment, so a guarantee that does not provide you with any protection of the value of your annuity while you are alive is not worth very much to you. Second, the insurance company will charge you dearly for the life insurance component of the annuity, which is referred to as a mortality expense charge (M&E). The cost of this life insurance component of your annuity is particularly high when compared to the protection you are receiving. If you need life insurance (and many of us do), buy life insurance. It does not present any great value in a variable annuity.

Variable annuities often appeal to people who want the opportunity for the gains that can be achieved through ownership of mutual funds, but want some guarantees. They want it both ways. Unfortunately, the only guarantees in a variable annuity protect your investment not for you, but for your heirs, so the guarantee is illusory.

As always when it comes to investing, the mantra you should repeat in your mind is that it is not what you make that counts, it is what you keep. And when it comes to variable annuities, the myriads of fees contained within the variable annuity drastically reduce what you get to keep. Start off with a regular account maintenance fee that you pay the insurance company for its regular administrative expenses related to your annuity, add a generous helping of sub-account management fees, sprinkle in a large dose of mortality and expense charges, and you have a lot of deductions before you ever end up making any money. And through the magic of accounting, these deductions come out of your earnings without being readily apparent to you. Of course, if you read the unreadable prospectus you received when you purchased the annuity, you would know all about these various fees.

And don't forget one of the worst potential fees of all: the surrender fee. If you need to cash in your annuity before the surrender period is up, you will be subject to extremely harsh fees that further reduce the value of your annuity.

It is also important to remember that once you start to take your money out of your annuity, you will be taxed not at the long-term capital gains rates that you would be charged if you took the same money out of a mutual fund you held outside of an annuity, but rather at higher ordinary income tax rates.

So why wouldn't you just buy mutual funds? The answer is that most people are probably better off just buying lower-cost mutual funds.

Just what are the benefits to buying variable annuities? Perhaps the biggest selling point for a variable annuity is that your investment grows tax-deferred. The value of income tax deferral is quite significant. And although you can achieve tax deferral in other investments such as a traditional IRA or a 401(k), the truth is that you are limited as to the amount you can invest in a traditional IRA or a 401(k). You have no such contribution limits with a deferred variable annuity. However, due to the overwhelming factors of fees and income taxes, you should maximize your traditional IRA or 401(k) before you consider buying an annuity.

Another interesting advantage of purchasing a deferred variable annuity is unusual in the sense that people who buy annuities are usually conservative investors who tend to hold on to their investments for long periods of time. However, if you are a more aggressive investor who is looking for the advantages of tax deferral, a deferred variable annuity may fit your needs. It allows you to switch your investments among the various mutual funds offered in your annuity without incurring the income taxes you would have to pay if, in an effort to seek a higher return, you did such switching among mutual funds held outside of an annuity.

If a variable annuity is in your future, follow the sage words of investment guru Smokey Robinson and shop around. Fees are such a significant matter when it comes to the suitability of annuities that it makes sense to seek out annuities from good companies with low fees. They are out there, but you need to do your homework.

TRUTH 7

Variable annuity investment choices

"*Life is the sum of all of your choices.*"

—Voltaire

Although Voltaire most likely was not referring to annuities, perhaps nowhere is his observation truer than when it comes to choosing the investments that make up the sub-accounts of your variable annuity. What you receive from your variable annuity is tied directly to the performance of the mutual fund sub-accounts you choose to be included in your annuity.

What you receive from your variable annuity is tied directly to the performance of the mutual fund sub-accounts you choose to be included in your annuity.

The specific choices among sub-accounts available to you will vary somewhat from annuity issuer to annuity issuer; however, they will pretty much fall into the general categories that I will describe. They may look familiar to you because they are the same types of investments that you will find offered by the mutual fund companies. In fact, the funds available to you in your annuity are offered by these same mutual fund companies, such as Fidelity, Franklin Templeton, Dreyfus, or Putnam. However, even though they look the same, they will differ in some degree from similar mutual funds offered by these same companies if you were to buy a mutual fund outside of your annuity, because the law requires that they not be identical.

Some of the types of funds from which you may choose include the following:

Aggressive growth funds—These are funds targeted at stock in companies that are believed to have the greatest potential for growth. Dividends are of no concern to the managers of aggressive growth funds. During Bull markets, these stocks generally do their best, and they are at their worst during Bear markets. If you are looking for a greater potential for gain, even though it is coupled with a greater potential for losses, this is your fund.

Growth funds—Not feeling particularly aggressive? Then this might be the sub-account for you. These sub-accounts look for companies that provide a potential for growth, but are coupled with some dividend income.

Balanced fund—This sub-account invests not just in stocks, but also in more secure and safe bonds. The relative percentage of the sub-account in stocks and bonds vary depending upon the fund manager's opinion as to the direction of the market.

Convertible funds—I have had a number of convertibles in my life and enjoyed riding in them. You may enjoy the ride that a convertible sub-account provides you, as well. Convertibles as an investment are convertible preferred stocks and bonds that permit the manager of the sub-account to convert the preferred stocks and bonds to common stock in the same company to take advantage of rising prospects within the company. During times that are less favorable, the manager keeps the preferred stocks and bonds in the company that may pay a higher dividend or interest rate than would be found in the company's common stock at that particular time.

Utilities—These sub-accounts invest in companies that provide electricity, water, gas, and phone services. These are all services that, regardless of the economic times, people still need. They are a conservative investment, but like the little engine that could, they always seem to chug away.

Corporate bonds—These sub-accounts hold commercial papers, which are bonds, issued by companies to raise money. They may be short-term or long-term bonds depending upon their maturity date, which is the date when the issuer of the bond must pay back the face value of the bond, and at which time, it stops paying interest. When interest rates are rising, the values of bonds go down, and conversely when interest rates are going down, the value of bonds increase. The longer the time remaining until maturity of the bond, the more pronounced is this effect on the bond's value.

Government bonds—Our government and its agencies are always borrowing money. If you invest in one of these sub-accounts, they can be borrowing from you. These bonds may be short term with maturities of 5 years or less, intermediate with maturities of between 5 and 15 years, or long term with maturities of more than 15 years. Just like with corporate bonds, the value of these bonds are affected by changes in the interest rates. However, when it comes to security and safety of your investment, it is hard to beat the federal government.

High yield bonds—For some people, high yield bonds is just another way of saying junk bonds, but in essence these are bonds that offer the potential for greater return on your investment than ordinary corporate bonds, but also carry a higher risk of defaulting. In fact, that is one of the reasons some of these companies offer higher interest rates because they have to do so in order to attract investment dollars. Some of the companies offering high yield bonds are not particularly strong companies with great prospects, but others may just be young companies without a sufficient track record to warrant being able to borrow money at lower interest rates.

International funds—Much economic growth is occurring in countries such as China, India, and other countries experiencing rapid expansion of their economies. These sub-accounts invest in these emerging markets and have, in recent years, had handsome returns on their investments. Will this continue? Your guess is as good as theirs.

Global bonds—Just as you can invest in the stocks of companies in foreign countries through International Fund sub-accounts, so can you also invest in these foreign companies' bonds through this kind of sub-account.

Precious metals—Some people are happiest when there is gold in them thar sub-accounts. And the insurance companies issuing annuities are only happy to provide precious metal sub-accounts that invest in gold, silver, and other precious metals.

So what does it cost you?

Just as you would pay a management fee if you owned these sub-accounts as mutual funds outside of your annuity, you also will pay a management fee for owning these sub-accounts within your annuity. The truth is that in some instances, the management fees may be even less for the sub-accounts in your annuity than what you would pay for similar accounts if you owned them outside of your annuity. Of course, you could always look for an annuity issued by one of the mutual fund companies, such as Vanguard, that offers much lower fees including reduced management fees. And remember: the less you pay in fees, the more money you have working for you.

TRUTH 8

Actively managing variable annuity sub-accounts

"Retirement is like a long vacation in Las Vegas. The goal is to enjoy it to the fullest, but not so fully that you run out of money."

—Jonathan Clements

Although annuities are anything but simple, many people buy them because they see them as a simple way of investing in a tax-deferred investment. Variable annuities with their various mutual fund-like sub-accounts permit investors to save for a long-term goal such as retirement in a tax-deferred vehicle that combines the advantages of tax deferral with the advantages of long-term investing in the stock and bond markets.

The return on your investment in a variable annuity is directly tied to the performance of the sub-accounts that make up your annuity. Many people who do not have confidence in their ability to choose among investments leave the determination as to which sub-accounts are appropriate for them, particularly considering their age and risk tolerance, to professional money managers within their variable annuity. They rely on these money managers to make the decisions as to where the money in their variable annuity should best be invested. Of course, they pay for this service, just as they would if they were to receive investment management services outside of an annuity.

But other people look at their variable annuity as combining a unique opportunity to invest in the stock and bond markets with the ability to shift money from one investment to another without having to pay an income tax on the profits of individual sales of investments—in this case, money invested in the variable annuity's sub-accounts. If you had invested in a similar portfolio of mutual funds outside of an annuity, you would be required to pay income taxes on profits realized when you sell shares of your various mutual funds in order to maintain a balanced portfolio. In a variable annuity, you can rebalance your portfolio of sub-accounts through buying and selling of shares without incurring any income tax.

But why do you need to rebalance your account?

In a variable annuity, you can rebalance your portfolio of sub-accounts through buying and selling of shares without incurring any income tax.

When you initially purchase a variable annuity, your investments within the annuity will be a mix of sub-account investments that are consistent with your investing philosophy, your age, and your tolerance for risk. Balancing your portfolio among various kinds of investments provides you with a much greater chance to maximize not only the income potential of your portfolio, but also the growth potential as well. A balanced portfolio will never earn the gains of a portfolio invested in the hot sector of the moment—be it technology stocks, foreign stocks, or whatever—but it will insulate you from the inevitable, difficult-to-predict downturns when the hot sector of the moment suddenly turns cold. By balancing your sub-accounts among a proper variety of different types of investments, you will be able to achieve steady growth without the fear of a dramatic loss in value of your portfolio. You minimize the risk you would have if all of your money were invested in a single segment of the market. You will have spread out your bets among almost all of the horses in the race, so no matter who wins, you have a bet on the right horse.

But keeping your balance requires rebalancing at regular intervals to ensure that you are maintaining the proper asset allocation for you. Although it rarely makes sense to rebalance your portfolio by changing the proportions of your investments in particular sub-accounts too often, it does make sense to rebalance your sub-account portfolio on a regular basis, such as once or twice a year. In this way, as some aspects of your investment portfolio become a greater portion of your total portfolio, you may find it reasonable to reallocate your assets in order to maintain the desired proportions you initially determined when making your original asset allocation. For instance, you may wish to have 65% of your portfolio in growth stocks and 35% of your

Although it rarely makes sense to rebalance your portfolio by changing the proportions of your investments in particular sub-accounts too often, it does make sense to rebalance your sub-account portfolio on a regular basis.

portfolio in bonds. If your growth stocks have had particular success this year, they may now constitute 75% of your portfolio. In that instance, it may well be in your best interest, in order to maintain the asset allocation strategy that is most appropriate for you, to sell some of your growth stock sub-account shares and put that money into your bond sub-accounts to preserve your particular appropriate asset allocation. In a variable annuity, you can do this without incurring income taxes.

Dollar cost averaging

Another common strategy for investing both inside and outside of a variable annuity is dollar cost averaging. With dollar cost averaging, on a regular basis—be it weekly, monthly, or whatever—you invest the same amount (in this case, in your variable annuity sub-accounts). During times when the markets or the segments of the market in which you are investing are low, your dollar cost averaged dollars will buy more shares, while during times in which the market or the segments of the market in which you are investing are high, your regular investment dollars will buy fewer shares. The idea behind dollar cost averaging is that by avoiding trying to do the impossible and buy at the optimum moments when prices are at their lowest, you put yourself in a position where you will be buying when stocks are both low and high, but by doing so will avoid missing out on buying opportunities. No one can predict the stock market. With dollar cost averaging, you do not try to predict the stock market. You take the emotionalism out of investing, and that is always a good thing. There may be some controversy as to whether dollar cost averaging actually is the soundest of investment strategies; however, there is no doubt that regular disciplined investment over time will ultimately work greatly to your advantage.

TRUTH 9

Equity indexed annuities

"The four most dangerous words in investing are 'This time it's different.'"

—John Templeton

Investors in annuities quite often are people who are not risk takers. They are concerned about the security of their investments. But many conservative investors would still like a shot at the opportunity for higher rewards made possible by investing in the stock market, but are fearful of inevitable stock market downturns. It is to these people that insurance companies have targeted Equity Indexed Annuities.

An Equity Indexed Annuity is a fixed annuity—it offers a guaranteed interest rate during the accumulation period, which is the period from the time that the investor invests his or her money in the annuity until the time that he or she begins to take money out of the annuity. Similar to other fixed annuities, an Equity Indexed Annuity contains provisions which guarantee that the insurance company will pay you a minimum interest rate (usually about 3%). Unlike the more standard fixed annuity, however, the interest rate is not at a fixed rate set by the insurance company, but rather is connected to the movement of the particular underlying index to which your annuity is tied, such as the Dow Jones Industrial Average or the S & P 500. It would appear that you get the benefits of upturns in the stock market without the risk of downturns. It may appear that way, but the fine print makes this no sure thing. So, let's look at the fine print.

Participation rates

Although you might assume that with an Equity Indexed Annuity, you will get the full benefit of any increases in the value of the underlying indexes that you choose for your annuity, you would be wrong. Within the fine print of your annuity contract is a provision that sets the Participation Rate, which specifies just how much of any increases in your particular underlying equity index is passed on to you. For example, if your participation rate is 80% and your particular index increases by 9%, you are credited with a gain of 7.2% (.80 × 9). You can find the Participation Rate for your particular annuity within the fine print of your annuity contract, but you may wish to keep reading after you have found it. In some Equity Indexed Annuities, the insurance company only guarantees the Participation Rate for a single year, whereas others may lock in the Participation Rate for the entire period of the Equity Indexed Annuity, which may be anywhere from five to ten years. Caveat Emptor.

What about dividends?

Never assume anything. A large part of the investment return of some stock indexes involves stock dividends. However, within the fine print of your Equity Indexed Annuity may be a provision which states that dividends are not considered in determining your payment under the terms of the annuity.

> Although you might assume that with an Equity Indexed Annuity, you will get the full benefit of any increases in the value of the underlying indexes that you choose for your annuity, you would be wrong.

Interest rate caps

Another unwelcome item found in the fine print of your Equity Indexed Annuity is the Interest Rate Cap. In addition to the reduced amount you receive when compared to the actual returns of the stock index you are using as a result of the Participation Rate in your annuity, some annuities also have Interest Rate Caps that limit the interest rate the insurance company will pay you, regardless of increases in the underlying index. For example, if your Interest Rate Cap is 10%, that is the top rate you will receive, regardless of the fact that the underlying stock index in your annuity may have gone up 20% during the year.

Margin—spread—asset fees—administration fees

If it walks like a duck and quacks like a duck, it is most likely a duck—unless, of course, if it is a goose. However, regardless of the name the insurance company gives it—margin fees, spread fees, asset fees, or administration fees—they all represent the same thing: other fees that reduce the amount you stand to gain from your Equity Indexed Annuity. For example, if your annuity has an administration fee of 3% and the underlying index went up by 8%, the return actually credited to you is only 5%. This fee may be assessed in lieu of a Participation Rate provision. However, some insurance companies have Equity Indexed Annuities that charge both fees. Remember, not all Equity Indexed Annuities are created equally.

Make sure you understand all fees and costs, both actual and potential, when you compare Equity Indexed Annuities of different companies.

Simple or compound interest

It is a simple concept to overlook, but whether or not your Equity Indexed Annuity pays you interest on a simple interest basis or a compound interest basis can have a significant effect on what you stand to gain from your Equity Indexed Annuity. With compound interest, the interest that you earn during one period is added to the principal of your annuity; so during the next period, you are earning interest on not just your initial principal, but also the interest from the preceding period. Thus, you get interest on interest. The IRS and banks have developed this concept into an art when you pay overdue taxes or your monthly mortgage payment, but it can work to your favor in your Equity Indexed Annuity if you know enough to look for this provision when comparing annuities.

Early withdrawal fees

Generally, if you cash in all or a portion of your Equity Indexed Annuity before the term of the annuity is up, you will be subject to financial penalties in the form of surrender fees or withdrawal charges, which usually are a percentage of the amount you are cashing out of the annuity. Fortunately, the withdrawal charge may go down or even be eliminated altogether during the latter years of the annuity. As always, this varies from company to company, so you should look for this provision when comparing annuities. You should also scan the fine print to see if the insurance company penalizes you if you take an early withdrawal by failing to give you credit for any or only a portion of the underlying index's increase in value. Some Equity Indexed Annuities provide for a period of early withdrawal without a penalty during each year of the annuity's term. There are limitations on the amount that you may withdraw without penalty. Generally, if you need the money from your annuity because of a terminal illness or you are going to a nursing home, the insurance companies will waive their early withdrawal fees.

TRUTH 10

More about equity indexed annuities

"There's no business like show business, but there are several businesses like accounting."

—David Letterman

One of the obviously key elements in any Equity Indexed Annuity is the particular stock market index used to determine the income to be earned from the specific annuity that you choose. Many of us are already familiar with the various indexes used as a measuring rod of Equity Indexed Annuities. What follows are some of the most commonly used indexes.

Dow Jones Industrial Average

Perhaps the most familiar, but not necessarily well-understood, stock index is the Dow Jones Industrial Average. This originated in 1896 and was made up of only 12 companies, including such stalwarts as American Cotton Oil and Laclede Gas Light Company. Laclede Gas Light Company also has the distinction to be the first stock dropped from the index. Over the years, this portfolio of now 30 stocks has changed, with companies being dropped and others added in an attempt to reflect the stock market in general. One company that has made it from the very first index to today is General Electric, which still seems to have a lot of energy left in it. The most recent changes in the Dow occurred in 2004, when Pfizer, Verizon, and AIG replaced International Paper, AT &T, and Eastman Kodak. A good question might by why such reliance is given to this one list of only 30 stocks as being representative of the entire broad stock market. The answer may be that it has managed to stand the test of time just by sheer staying power, but that doesn't mean that there may not be better indexes for measuring the general stock market.

The S & P 500 uses the stocks of 500 leading companies to measure the stock market rather than only the 30 companies that make up the Dow Jones Industrial Average.

S & P 500

The most popular index for Equity Indexed Annuities is the S & P 500 Index. S & P 500 stands for Standard and Poor's. Poor is certainly not a word you want associated with your investments, which may be why the index is most commonly referred to by the initials S & P. In any event, the S & P 500 Index is thought by many to be a better measure of the overall stock market and economy than the Dow Jones Industrial Average. For one thing, the S & P 500 uses the stocks of 500 leading companies to measure the stock market rather than only the 30 companies that make up the Dow Jones Industrial Average.

Nasdaq 100

The Nasdaq 100 is another popular index that is of recent origin, having only been around since 1985. The Nasdaq 100 is largely made up of younger and more high-tech companies than the Dow Jones Industrial Average. It also contains companies incorporated in foreign countries as well as the United States, while the Dow Jones Industrial Average only includes American companies.

Russell 2000 Index

Another popular index is the Russell 2000 Index, which consists of the stocks of 2,000 smaller companies, thereby giving investors a chance to participate in the growth potential of companies with smaller capitalization. Small is a relative term, and these "small" or "small cap" companies may indeed be small when compared to the market cap of a behemoth such as General Electric with a market cap in excess of 400 billion dollars. But they are not that small when you consider that the average capitalization of a company in the Russell 2000 index is about 530 million dollars. By the way, market capitalization represents the value of all the stock in a particular company. It is calculated by multiplying the price of one share of the particular company's stock by the total number of outstanding shares in the company.

How can I lose with an Equity Indexed Annuity?

With Equity Indexed Annuities, you get a guaranteed rate of return and the apparent ability to share in rises in value of the stock market without the risk of taking the losses that come with falls in the stock market. In fact, Equity Indexed Annuities are often thought of as foolproof. But never underestimate the power of a fool. Although actually losing money in an Equity Indexed Annuity is not likely, it

Equity Indexed Annuities should only be considered by people who have absolutely no intention of possibly cashing in the annuity before its full term has expired.

is not impossible, as some of the sellers of these annuities would have you believe. Like all annuities, they come with fees. Lots of fees. Start off with the fact that unlike more common fixed annuities, with an Equity Indexed Annuity, your initial payment for the annuity is not 100% guaranteed. So, if the stock market falls, your 3% guaranteed interest rate may not be enough to provide you with enough money to cover your initial investment—particularly if you cash in the policy early and are subject to substantial surrender fees designed to discourage early cashing in of the annuity that can be in effect for as long as you own the annuity. The bottom line is that Equity Indexed Annuities should only be considered by people who have absolutely no intention of possibly cashing in the annuity before its full term has expired.

TRUTH 11

Calculating index changes

"Get your facts first, and then you can distort them as much as you please."

—Mark Twain

When determining the profitability of an Equity Indexed Annuity, it is important to consider what particular index will be used to determine your payments. As I have previously indicated, the most popular indexes are the S & P 500 Index, the Dow Jones Industrial Average, the Nasdaq 100, and the Russell 2000 Index. Equally as important to your ultimate goal of earning a profit on your investment is the method used by the issuer of your annuity to determine changes in the index. Although you might not think that this is important, in truth, it is of critical importance to you.

There are three primary methods used by insurance companies issuing annuities to measure change in the underlying index that makes up the particular Equity Indexed Annuity that you may have. The first is the Annual Reset, which is sometimes referred to as the Ratchet. The second is the High Water Mark, and the third is the Point-to-Point method. As you might expect, each has advantages and disadvantages. It is also important not to look at these indexing methods in isolation, but rather as a part of the entire picture of fees, costs, and provisions that govern your annuity.

The *Annual Reset*, or Ratchet, is a simple concept. The insurance company merely compares the value of the particular index that is used in your annuity from the date that you purchased the annuity to the value of the index exactly one year later. The difference between these two figures is converted to a percentage. However, administrative fees reduce this percentage, and the participation rate and cap rate are further factored in before your interest rate is finally computed. At that time, the earnings from your account are locked in and a new base value for the index in the next year is determined. Because your gains are locked in during years in which the index rises, your profits are not reduced during years in which the index goes down. In fact, down years in the underlying index might well work to your advantage as market recoveries inevitably happen. If this looks pretty good to you, you are right—it is. Unfortunately, the insurance company often may compensate for this advantageous method of determining changes in the index by having lower participation rates, higher asset management fees, and lower interest caps than annuities utilizing a different indexing method. You generally will be better off with a higher participation rate and should be less concerned with a lower cap rate because historically over the last fifty years, stocks have averaged annual increases of 12%. Getting a higher percentage of profit in years in which the index rises as much as 15% is ultimately more likely to provide you with more value than being able to chase after the very high profits in those uncommon years in which the index rises by 20% or more.

Getting a higher percentage of profit in years in which the index rises as much as 15% is ultimately more likely to provide you with more value than being able to chase after the very high profits in those uncommon years in which the index rises by 20% or more.

The *High Water Mark* method compares the value of the index annually for each year of the annuity's duration and measures the change from the time that you first purchased the annuity. For example, a five-year annuity that had its high point in value at the time of the measurement at the end of the second year would use that value to compute the interest rate for the annuity. The obvious advantage to this index measurement is that it is pretty likely that sometime during the term of your annuity, there will be a year with a substantial profit, which puts you in good stead for your rate of return on your annuity. The bad news, however, is that some annuities using this measuring method do not provide you with the benefit of any raises in the index rate if you surrender the annuity prematurely, although some companies do provide some credit for some partial interest. Again, you should be on the lookout for how this index measurement matches up with the other fees and provisions contained in your annuity, such as lower participation rates or higher management fees. Fortunately, with this method of index measurement, there is no cap rate. So if the market manages to have a bang-up year and achieves gains of 35%, you will, depending on your participation rate and management fees, get a large part of that increase. You get the most bang for your buck when the index reaches a high early in the term of the annuity, but it is a pretty good measurement in most situations if it is not paired with too many limiting provisions and fees within your annuity.

The *Point-to-Point* indexing method merely compares the value of the account on the day you purchased the annuity to the value at the end of the term of the annuity. This difference in value is reduced to a percentage and then applied to your account to determine what you will get. Generally, because interest is not credited to your annuity until the end of the term of the annuity, early surrender of the annuity may bring no interest at all. In addition, because it only measures two days out of the entire term of the annuity, you run the substantial risk of buying the annuity on a day that the index was high and ending the annuity on a particular day that the index is low. However, this indexing method typically carries the highest participation rate, and if the market does rise during the time that you have the annuity, you stand to make a significant gain.

Forgetting for a moment the effect of fees and other annuity contract provisions on the amount of your profit, which one of these three index measurements is best for you? It depends on how the stock markets in general and your particular index of stocks fare during the time you have the annuity.

The Annual Reset method works best during average periods where the market does not move tremendously, although it can also work quite well during periods when there is a dramatic drop during a single year that is recovered in the year or two following the down year.

The High Water Mark method works best during periods of tremendous volatility, when the market may have sharp upswings and downswings. Because your ultimate profit is tied to the highest level of the index attained during the annuity period, you are more concerned with the highs than the lows.

The Point-to-Point method works best in extended Bull markets with a large number of good years throughout the annuity period.

TRUTH 12

Inflation-protected annuities

"A nickel ain't worth a dime anymore."

—Yogi Berra

What do you fear the most? Spiders, snakes, lawyers? Inflation is at the top of the list for many retirees. The fear that their money will not last as long as they do is of great concern to many older Americans. And to some extent, it is a realistic fear. Even relatively small inflation can eat away at the purchasing power of your investments and make your retirement much more challenging. In the 1990s, the rate of inflation was around 3%; in the 1980s, it was around 5%, and in the 1970s, it was around 7%. In 2007 the inflation rate was under 3%, yet the fear remains. Although inflation is not something to fear, it certainly is something to consider. At a steady 3% inflation rate, $1,000 today will only be worth $859 in 5 years. After 20 years, that $1,000 will only be worth $544, which is a frightening proposition to many older Americans.

Therein lies the problem. Many seniors are conservative investors, so they invest in safe, secure investments like Certificates of Deposit and Treasury bills. These are certainly not very exciting investments, but people who consider themselves unsophisticated investors, and perhaps rightfully so, are comfortable with these particular investments. Unfortunately, although these investments are safe and secure by definition, no fixed investment—an investment that returns a specific amount of interest—is ever an effective hedge against inflation because the interest rate earned by your investment does not rise as inflation rises and eats into the buying power of your investment.

No fixed investment—an investment that returns a specific amount of interest—is ever an effective hedge against inflation.

Once again, where others see a problem, the insurance industry sees an opportunity. They know that many older people find the lure of an immediate annuity that will provide lifetime income very attractive. Yet both retirees and the insurance companies recognize that a fixed immediate annuity purchased by a retiree is just another investment that pays a fixed rate, and even if it will provide a steady income for the rest of the annuity owner's life, it will not keep pace with inflation. So the insurance companies developed another new wrinkle for annuities for those of us with wrinkles of our own—inflation-protected annuity. This is an annuity that ties the payments to inflation, although generally there is a cap, such as 10%. On the surface, this would seem to have a great deal of appeal by combining both the security of regular payments for the rest of your life with an adjustment of your payment for inflation. Unfortunately, like everything in this world, it comes at a price. The cost to the purchaser of an inflation-protected annuity is higher than an annuity that does not provide this protection. However, the initial payments from the inflation-protected annuity can be as much as 30% lower than the payments provided by a plain vanilla, fixed immediate annuity.

The cost to the purchaser of an inflation-protected annuity is higher than an annuity that does not provide this protection. The initial payments from the inflation-protected annuity can be as much as 30% lower than the payments provided by a plain vanilla, fixed immediate annuity.

Is it worth it? It is true that inflation represents a real threat to people's retirement, but is it that bad and is an inflation-protected annuity the answer?

The answer for most people is probably not. The difference in the cost of an inflation-protected annuity relative to the benefits it brings are such that it could take 20 years before you come out ahead of a fixed immediate annuity. In addition, the primary way to combat inflation is to invest in the stock market. Investing in low-cost index mutual funds is a relatively safe way to participate in the growth that has occurred regularly over time in the stock market and which we have every reason to believe will continue to grow. In addition, you could consider investing in Treasury Inflation-Protected Securities (TIPS), which are offered by the United States Treasury, so you know they are a safe and secure investment. TIPS are bonds that pay a specific interest rate; however, when the Consumer Price Index increases, the Treasury adjusts the interest rate of your bond accordingly in order to keep up with inflation.

So what is the best way to get the best of both worlds: protection from inflation and a steady stream of income for the rest of your life?

Instead of paying higher fees for the initially lesser returns of an inflation-protected annuity, you might consider splitting your money at retirement and putting some of it into a safe and secure fixed immediate annuity and some of it in the stock market by investing in low-cost index mutual funds. If you are feeling particularly venturesome, you might even consider putting some of your money into gold or other precious metals that generally do better as inflation rises. The fixed immediate annuity will provide you with a safe, steady stream of income for the rest of your life. It may be plain vanilla, but plain vanilla tastes pretty good sometimes, particularly if you are risk adverse and want to have at least a portion of your retirement income guaranteed. And, working in your favor is the fact that the older you are when you buy the fixed immediate annuity, the more money you receive. If inflation is a concern to you, waiting until you are older makes sense because if your life expectancy is not particularly long, you do not have to worry as much about long-term inflation. There is no downside to waiting until you retire to buy the annuity. In addition, by putting off buying the annuity until you retire, you assure yourself of getting the then-current interest rates. If you are concerned about possibly dying young, you can buy an annuity that pays you for life, but also has a term-certain so that even if you die prematurely, your heirs will receive the benefits of your annuity for the remainder of the specific term you chose, such as 10 or 15 years.

Meanwhile, the money that you invest in mutual funds will help protect you against the ravages of inflation. As always, it is not what you make that is important, it is what you keep. By combining a low-cost fixed immediate annuity with low-cost index mutual funds, you will be in a better position to balance your risk and reward. You also will not only protect your retirement income from inflation, but do so at less cost so that more of your money actually is working for you throughout your retirement.

TRUTH 13

Tax-sheltered annuities

"In this world, nothing can be said to be certain, except death and taxes."

—Benjamin Franklin

Say the acronym TSA, and many people will think about the Transportation Security Administration and long lines at airport security checkpoints. However, say TSA to a teacher, a hospital worker, a self-employed minister, or an employee of an Native American tribal government, and TSA may have a much different meaning. To them, the term means tax-sheltered annuity.

A TSA is an annuity that is contained in a 403(b) plan. The 403(b) is the equivalent of a 401(k) for people who work for school systems, hospitals, or other non-profit charitable institutions. Like a 401(k), your contribution to a 403(b) is limited. In fact, the limits are exactly the same as those for a 401(k). As with a 401(k), people over the age of 50 are able to make larger "catch-up" contributions to their 403(b) accounts. Also, like a 401(k), your 403(b) plan may provide not only for you to contribute a portion of your salary before taxes to the retirement plan, but you may also have a matching contribution paid by your employer to your TSA.

Congress created the 403(b) plan in 1958. At that time, the only investment that could be contained within it was an annuity. Now, as with 401(k) accounts, you can invest your 403(b) in mutual funds, although most people who participate in 403(b) plans still choose annuities as their investment of choice. For many of them, the attraction of an annuity is, as it has always been, the fact that unlike any other investment, an annuity can offer a guaranteed stream of income for the rest of your life. Indeed, there may be a place in your 403(b) for a fixed annuity. However, whether you are buying a variable annuity inside a 403(b) or purchasing one individually outside of a qualified retirement plan, the fees associated with many variable annuities do not make them a very good choice for most people. Unfortunately, many people who do not understand the investment options available to them in their 403(b) often choose annuities almost by default or because salesmen steer them into an investment that may be better for the salesman than the client.

The fees associated with many variable annuities do not make them a very good choice for most people.

The money in your TSA continues to grow tax-deferred in either a fixed annuity or a variable annuity. As with all variable annuities, you have the opportunity to get a greater return on your investment if the stock market in general—and the sub-accounts that you pick in particular—do well; but conversely you stand to not do well if your picks are less than stellar. In addition, all of the concerns about the fees for variable annuities being too high are present with a variable annuity that is a TSA within a 403(b). In addition, as with all annuities, some of the fees may be apparent to you, but others are hidden and are done in a manner that they reduce your profits, but are not readily disclosed to you on a regular basis so that you may not even be aware of them.

Like a 401(k), your investment in a 403(b) grows tax-deferred, which means that once you start to take money out of your 403(b), you will pay income taxes on the money that you take. As with a 401(k) account, there are limitations on your access to the money in your account without a penalty for withdrawals before the age of 59 ½. You can take out money from your TSA before retirement in the event of certain emergencies or when the employer establishing the 403(b) no longer employs you. In that event, you may be able to transfer your 403(b) to a plan with your new employer or to an IRA.

Another characteristic that 403(b) accounts share with 401(k)s is the ability to borrow from your 403(b), although not all TSAs permit such borrowing. In any event, borrowing from a 401(k) or a 403(b) is rarely an advisable move. Borrowing from a TSA within your 403(b) is not only highly regulated and limited by the IRS, but it also brings a host of new fees that you must pay. And perhaps most significantly, when you are borrowing from your TSA, you are reducing the amount of money that would otherwise be growing for you on a tax-deferred basis.

At retirement, you have a number of different options for your TSA. The first is to do nothing at all and just let the TSA continue to grow so that you can withdraw money from the TSA at a later date. You can also transfer the TSA to an annuity with another insurer or you can move the money into an IRA. In addition, as the name implies, you can choose to annuitize your annuity and take out the money over the period of your choice. You may choose to take out the money over your projected lifetime or you may choose a joint and survivor

The primary advantage, however, to purchasing an annuity inside a 403(b) is that this is the only time you can buy an annuity with pretax money, and that is a significant advantage.

option or a period-certain. (For more information on the kinds of choices available to you, see Chapter 14, "Annuity Settlement Options.")

Ultimately, an annuity within a 403(b) carries the same advantages and disadvantages as an annuity outside of a 403(b). And although there is no limit to the amount that you can contribute to an annuity outside of a qualified plan, you are subject to limitations on the amount you can invest in a TSA within a qualified 403(b) plan. The primary advantage, however, to purchasing an annuity inside a 403(b) is that this is the only time you can buy an annuity with pretax money, and that is a significant advantage. So if a fixed annuity is your cup of tea, a TSA within a qualified 403(b) is a good teahouse.

TRUTH 14

Annuity settlement options

"Simplify, simplify, simplify."

—Henry David Thoreau

Very little about annuities are simple, and the various ways you can receive your money from an annuity is not an exception to this rule.

Lifetime-only payout

Perhaps the most basic form of an annuity payout is the option to take your payments in regular payments, usually monthly, for the rest of your life regardless of how long you may live. This is a particularly attractive option for people who need as much income as they can squeeze from their annuities and are not concerned about leaving money from their annuities for their children or others. Although this particular payout option provides for the highest payout, it also terminates at the death of the annuitant with nothing available to be paid to anyone else. The upside is if you live a long life, you end up making a particularly good deal because the insurance company must pay you for as long as you live. However, the potential downside is that if you die prematurely, such as a month after you buy the annuity, everything left in the annuity passes to the insurance company. Like many gambles, you may win big or lose big. However, you may have an edge if you have longevity in your family and maintain a healthy lifestyle. In any event, if you have children or others that you want to inherit your wealth, a lifetime-only payout may not be worth the little you may gain in your lifetime payments.

Lifetime refund annuity

This option is similar to the lifetime-only payout with the significant exception that if you die before you have received back the original purchase price of your annuity, your designated beneficiary will receive the balance of any remaining initial premium either in regular installments or in a lump sum. For instance, if someone paid $200,000 for an annuity, but had received only $50,000 in payments before dying, the annuity would pay the remaining $150,000 of the initial premium either in regular monthly or quarterly payments or a lump sum to the beneficiary designated by the annuity owner. As you might expect, this option comes at a cost. In this case, it is lower monthly payments to the annuitant than he would receive in the lifetime-only payout, which provides the highest payout of all.

Lifetime payout with period certain annuity

This is another variation of the lifetime-only payout. In this case, the insurance company promises to pay the annuity payments for a specific period of time regardless of whether the original annuitant dies within the designated period. In the event that the original annuitant does die during the designated period, the insurance company will continue payments for the remainder of the chosen period to the designated beneficiary. People choosing this option generally may choose from among five-, ten-, fifteen-, or twenty-year periods. So, if the original owner of the annuity had an annuity with a fifteen-year certain period and died only two years into the annuity period, the designated beneficiary would receive the annuity payments for the next thirteen years.

Joint and survivor annuities

Because many of the purchasers of annuities are married couples, the joint and survivor options for annuity payments are popular. Under the terms of this annuity payment option, a husband and wife, for instance, may guarantee payments throughout both of their lifetimes. As you would imagine, the monthly payments from the annuity are determined, in part, by the ages of the two people involved.

With one variation of this payout option, the surviving annuitant continues to receive the same monthly payment as was being received before the death of the first spouse to die. Another variation of this payout option provides for a reduced monthly payout after the death of one of the annuitants. This amount, chosen by the annuitant at the time the annuity is purchased, may be anywhere from 50% to 75% of the former monthly payment amount. This type of option might be particularly appropriate if there was sufficient life insurance to compensate for the reduced income received from the annuity.

Because many of the purchasers of annuities are married couples, the joint and survivor options for annuity payments are popular.

Yet another variation of a joint and survivor annuity payout occurs when there is a primary annuitant and a backup contingent annuitant who receives payments only if the primary annuitant dies, as compared to the situation in the previous paragraph where there are two co-annuitants. With this particular payout option, the amount that is received pursuant to the annuity is reduced by the agreed-upon percentage only if the primary annuitant dies. If the contingent annuitant dies first, there is no reduction in the payments pursuant to the annuity to the primary annuitant.

More bells and whistles

There are even more variations of joint and survivor annuity payouts from among which purchasers of annuities may choose that add premium refund or payments for period-certain provisions to the annuity contract. Through these add-on provisions, you can guarantee that you or the people of your choice will profit from the ownership of your annuity at least to the extent of the money that you put into the annuity. Of course, for every bell and for every whistle, there is another fee. This is not to say that these variations may not represent the most appropriate payout provisions for some people. It is only to say that you must carefully compare the cost of these provisions to the benefit that you are likely to receive.

Comparisons

To illustrate what these various payment options would mean in dollars and cents to you, what follows is a comparison of the monthly payouts of various options for a 65-year-old man paying $100,000 for an immediate annuity in Massachusetts:

Lifetime-only payout with no payment to beneficiaries: $672

Lifetime payout with installment refund to beneficiaries: $632

Lifetime payout with 5-year term certain to beneficiaries: $667

Lifetime payout with 10-year term certain to beneficiaries: $649

Joint Life (100% to the survivor): $577

Joint Life (100% to the survivor) with up to 15 years to beneficiaries: $572

You can work out your own estimates to see how different settlement options would affect the money you would receive from a particular annuity by inputting your information at www.immediateannuities.com.

TRUTH 15

Tax deferral

"Never put off till tomorrow what you can do the day after tomorrow."

—Mark Twain

Mark Twain's advice is something that many of us procrastinators take to heart. Although often it may not be in your best interest to delay things, one thing that generally works in your favor is to delay or defer having to pay income taxes.

By not paying taxes on the earnings of any investment, what you achieve is having more money available to grow and compound. In effect, in addition to the principal that you invested originally, your earnings get added to that principal to be the basis of your future growth without any dilution. The longer you are able to have your money compound and grow without being reduced by the payment of income taxes, the more money you will ultimately be left with.

A familiar way of illustrating the value of compound interest is through what is known as the "Rule of 72." The Rule of 72 is a formula for estimating the time it would take for an investment to double in value. In its simplest form, the Rule of 72 takes the number 72 and divides it by the growth rate, which then gives you the number of years it will take to double your money at that particular growth rate if that growth rate is compounded. For example, if you invest $1,000 in an investment that provides you with 7% interest, your $1,000 investment would become worth $2,000 in a little over 10 years. The formula is a nice, easy way to estimate the value of compound growth. But a major assumption of the Rule of 72 is that the money you invest will not be reduced each year by the amount of income tax you would be required to pay if your investment was subject to yearly income tax payments.

Tax deferral is the most valuable aspect of a deferred annuity, and it should be obvious that the longer you are able to defer paying taxes on your investment, the greater the growth. This is one reason why, in order to be a truly effective investment, an annuity should be considered a long-term investment so that you can take the utmost advantage of the value of tax-deferred, compound growth.

The longer you are able to defer paying taxes on your investment, the greater the growth.

Let's look at an example of what tax-deferred, compound growth would mean in dollars and cents. Assume that you invest $10,000 and receive a consistent 6% growth rate each year. If you are in the low federal tax bracket of 15% and also have a typical 5% state income tax, after 30 years your investment of $10,000 would grow to a tidy $40,817. If you were paying taxes at 35% for your federal taxes and 5% for your state income taxes, your initial $10,000 investment would have increased, but only to $28,893 after 30 years. However, if instead of having income taxes eat into your profits, your investment continued to grow and compound tax deferred, your $10,000 investment would be worth $57,435 after 30 years. Obviously, the longer you can put off paying taxes, the more your money has an opportunity to grow. And the higher your present income tax brackets are during the period when income taxes are being deferred, the greater the benefit to you in the long run. Tax deferral is, as Martha Stewart would say, a good thing.

The higher your present income tax brackets are during the period when income taxes are being deferred, the greater the benefit to you in the long run.

There comes a time in any tax-deferred investment that you ultimately have to pay taxes. Some investments, most commonly a Roth IRA, grow totally tax-free and come out tax-free. This is one reason why a Roth IRA is superior to an annuity. But there are limitations as to who is eligible for a Roth IRA and how much you may invest each year. With annuities, there are no such limitations. You can invest as much as you want, and you do not need to meet any financial eligibility requirements in order to buy an annuity and avail yourself of its tax-deferral qualities. Although tax deferral is certainly not as valuable as a tax-free investment, it still presents a tremendous investing opportunity.

But then comes the tax. You get to choose when to pay the income tax because you are not taxed on the earnings of your annuity until you decide to take the money out of your annuity. As many people do, you may choose to take the money out of your annuity at retirement when your other sources of income may be less and your income tax bracket may be lower. However, the most negative aspect of the income taxation of annuity withdrawals is that you are taxed at your ordinary income tax rates. If you are in the 28% tax bracket, you will pay federal income taxes at the ordinary income tax rate of 28% on many years' worth of earnings from your annuity. This may appear to be particularly onerous when compared to the federal income taxes paid by someone who, instead of having his money invested in a variable annuity with underlying mutual fund-like investments, invested directly in mutual funds similar to the ones that form the investment part of your annuity. People in the 25% federal income tax bracket or higher would pay capital gains rates of only 15%, a significant drop from the income taxes that would be paid on essentially the same investment when an annuity is the investment vehicle of choice. However, the owner of the mutual fund would have been paying income taxes throughout the years, which would have reduced both the value of the investment and limited the amount of the assets that would be compounding over the years.

Also note that when opponents of annuities point out this significant difference in the tax rates to which annuities and other investments are assessed, they rarely indicate that these advantageous reduced capital gains income tax rates apply only to long-term capital gains where the investment was held for at least a year and a day. If the mutual fund sells a stock it has held less than a year and a day, the short-term capital gains tax rates apply to the sale. This gain is passed on to the mutual fund shareholders as an ordinary dividend subject to ordinary income tax rates. And over the years, investors in mutual funds pay income taxes at their ordinary income tax rates for non-qualified dividends, such as when the mutual fund receives taxable interest, but pays it out as a dividend to investors or when the mutual fund sells shares of a particular company that it has held for less than 61 days, during which time the mutual fund received a dividend related to the ownership of the particular stock.

TRUTH 16

Annuity risk

"The only thing we have to fear is fear itself."

—Franklin Roosevelt

For many people, the choice to purchase an annuity is one made out of fear—the fear that they will outlive their savings. Perhaps Franklin Roosevelt was right about fear. However, even if the only thing we have to fear is fear itself (not to mention tsunamis), piggy backing the fear that you will outlive your savings on top of the fear that your savings themselves are not safe is still a lot of fear.

The concern as to the safety of their savings is what drives many people, particularly those wary of the stock market, to Certificates of Deposit (CD)s. A good way to tell someone's age is to mention the acronym CD. If they immediately think of Certificates of Deposit, then they are most likely over 40. If instead, the first thing that comes to mind is a Compact Disc, you have someone under 40 who probably is not as concerned with safe investments.

The fear that you will outlive your savings on top of the fear that your savings themselves are not safe is a lot of fear.

CDs are as safe as money in the bank because that is exactly what they are. And even though it is not unheard of for a bank to fail, the federal government is there to rescue you through the Federal Deposit Insurance Corporation (FDIC), which insures your bank deposits up to $100,000. Many conservative CD holders, cognizant of this fact, will spread their savings among a number of banks to make sure that if any bank in which they have a CD goes under, rich Uncle Sam will come to the rescue.

Most people who consider purchasing an annuity have lived long enough to have seen repeated ups and downs in the stock market. They may recognize that there is much money and profit to be made in the stock market, but they also recognize that there seems to be a definite relationship between the risk that you are willing to accept and the possibility of reaping greater rewards. Many fearful or merely prudent investors are just not willing to take that risk. For although they know that history is on their side and that over time the stock market has always gone up in value, they are afraid of flunking history. They are afraid that they may not live long enough to have their losing investments in the stock market regain their luster.

It is fine to intellectually know that statistically over the past 50 years, the chances of making a profit in the stock market over any 10-year period is pretty much certain. However, emotionally, some people are either concerned that this record may not continue or that they may not have 10 years to invest their money.

No investment is a good one if it keeps you up at night worrying. So many people opt for safety. Groucho Marx was once asked what he invested in. To the surprise of the questioner, Groucho answered, "Treasury Bills." When told that you can't make money in Treasury Bills, Groucho merely replied that you could if you had enough of them. And indeed, Treasury Notes and Bills do offer a promising alternative to annuities. After all, when it comes to safety, nothing is safer than Treasury Notes and Bills, which are backed totally by the federal government. As Jerry Seinfeld said about the laundry detergent that proclaimed in its advertising that it was able to remove blood stains, "If you've got a T-shirt with a blood stain all over it, maybe laundry isn't your biggest problem." And so it is with Treasury Notes and Bills. The only scenario in which your Treasury Notes and Bills would not pay you is if the United States government were to fall, in which case you just might have bigger problems than your investments or your laundry.

At first blush, annuities may seem to be a more risky investment than CDs because annuities do not come with FDIC insurance, but are merely backed by the strength of the individual insurance company issuing the annuity. However, insurance companies issuing annuities are required by regulations in all states to have amounts set aside as "reserves" that, in some states, offer even greater protection than the limits of FDIC insurance. However, the bottom line always is that anytime you buy an annuity, the promise of the insurance company to pay you back with interest is only as secure as the insurance company itself. And it is for this reason that if you

Anytime you buy an annuity, the promise of the insurance company to pay you back with interest is only as secure as the insurance company itself.

purchase an annuity, one of the most important things with which you must concern yourself is the relative strength of the insurance company. This is particularly important because unlike some shorter-term investments, annuities are generally thought of as long-term investments. When you buy an annuity, you are looking forward to a relationship with the insurance company that you anticipate will endure for many years, which is all the more reason to make sure that the company with which you are dealing is a good, dependable one.

The good news is that there are a number of reliable rating services, such as A.M. Best, Standard & Poors, Moody's, and Weiss, which will provide you, at no cost, with ratings as to the strength and stability of the various insurance companies. All of these companies perform extensive evaluations of complex information to arrive at their conclusions. A.M. Best has been giving its best advice to consumers for more than a hundred years, ranking insurance companies according to their financial strength and their ability to meet their commitments to their policyholders, as well as their credit ratings. The bad news, however, is that their ratings are not consistent with each other and may be misleading if you merely look at the ratings out of context. A grade of B+ or A- might have been a good grade when you were in high school, but not when you are considering the strength of an insurance company selling you an annuity. An A- is only the fourth-highest rating for A.M. Best, the third-highest rating for Weiss, and the seventh-highest rating for Standard & Poors (talk about grade inflation). But so long as you make sure you understand the rating systems for each of these rating services, they can provide very useful information to help you evaluate the financial security of your annuity investment. You can find A.M. Best ratings at www.ambest.com, Standard & Poors at www.standardandpoors.com, Moody's at www.moodys.com, and Weiss at www.weissratings.com.

TRUTH 17

Annuity death benefits

“They say such nice things about people at their funerals that it makes me sad that I’m going to miss mine by just a few days.”

—Garrison Keillor

Whoopee! You die. You win. This concept is hard enough to comprehend when it comes to life insurance, but when it comes to annuity death benefits, it is even harder to make sense of, particularly if you read the fine print.

The death benefit found in a fixed annuity is actually pretty straightforward, as are most fixed annuities themselves. Many people consider fixed annuities as a conservative investment, much like a Certificate of Deposit that you would purchase at a bank. Like a CD, with a fixed annuity, you purchase the annuity from an insurance company, and the amount of interest that you are credited with is guaranteed at a certain rate for a specific number of years. It should be noted, however, that unlike a CD, the "fixed" rate you receive is not truly fixed for the entire time of your annuity. Rather, the insurance company may change that rate as it determines after the guarantee period within your annuity has expired.

In any event, the death benefit provision of a fixed annuity applies during the accumulation phase of the annuity. The accumulation phase is the period during which you are putting money into your annuity and before you start to regularly withdraw your principal and interest from the annuity. If you die during the accumulation phase, the insurance company will pay your beneficiary either what you paid into the annuity after deducting any previous withdrawals or the present value of the account, whichever is greater. However, with the conservative investments that form the basis of your fixed annuity, it is unlikely that the death benefit protects your estate from any significant risk of loss.

Unlike a CD, the "fixed" rate you receive is not truly fixed for the entire time of your annuity. Rather, the insurance company may change that rate as it determines after the guarantee period within your annuity has expired.

Annuity salesmen are quick to point out that your beneficiaries will receive the death benefit of your annuity quickly and that the value of the annuity death benefit will not be a part of the probate estate and the probate process. They are not as quick to point out that the death benefit is not treated the same way as life insurance, which is not subject to income tax. Although life insurance proceeds also generally pass to beneficiaries outside of probate, they also come income tax-free to the beneficiaries. With annuity death benefits, however, the gains in the annuity are not only subject to income taxes, but in addition, the income taxes that the gains are subject to are at higher ordinary income tax rates rather than lower capital gains rates.

The death benefit for a variable annuity is much more complicated than the death benefit contained in a fixed income annuity. At first look, the death benefit contained in a variable annuity would seem to provide a significant benefit because by guaranteeing to your beneficiaries during the accumulation phase of your annuity the greater of the amount of your contributions to the annuity or the value of the annuity, it would seem that you would have a valuable protection from any downturns in the stock market. For example, if you had invested $100,000 in a variable annuity and died during a time when the value of the sub-accounts contained in your annuity had dropped in value to $75,000, you would be guaranteed that your beneficiaries would receive the full $100,000 you had invested—minus, of course, some fees.

But at what cost?

Annual death benefit fees may start at around 1.1% of the value of your annuity, but go up to as much as 1.75% of the value of your annuity, depending on what options you choose in regard to the death benefit. If you purchased a $100,000 variable annuity and the mortality expense was 1.25% per year, you paid $1,250 per year for the death benefit. But are you really paying for $100,000 worth of life insurance? Because the amount of the death benefit is limited to the greater of the value of your account or what you paid for the annuity, the only way you are getting the equivalent of a $100,000 death benefit is if your account becomes totally worthless. Furthermore, if a 65-year-old healthy male were to purchase a $100,000 term life insurance policy, he could get one for as low as $580 per year, which is considerably less than the $1,250 per year he would be paying for the death benefit of his variable annuity; this would further reduce the benefits of the annuity to him while alive by reducing the amount of money actually earning him anything.

As always, there are many different variations of death benefits that each company offers in addition to the basic protection. One of these options is the Stepped-Up Death Benefit. With a Stepped-Up Death Benefit provision, you are able to lock in investment gains made during the life of your annuity. Under an Annual Step-Up, you may be able to lock in the highest value of your annuity each year as the amount protected by the death benefit. Under a Percentage Step-Up, the death benefit goes up by a specific percentage each year. It would appear that this offers some protection from inflation; but in fact, once again, if the stock market makes even minimal gains, the value of this option may be worthless if the regular death benefit would provide more of a death benefit due to the increase in value of your account and the increased fee for this death benefit.

Another optional variation on the death benefit that some people choose permits them to lock in the value of the account over a certain period, such as four years, for example. In this way, you would be able to lock in the increased value of your account every four years, and even if the market were down at the time of your death, you would be guaranteed the higher death benefit. A risk with this choice of death benefit option that may not be readily apparent is the concern that if the time of your review occurs during a year in which the stock market is down, you have gained nothing from this provision and its extra cost.

The truth is that death benefits sound much better than they play out. They come at a significant cost, and they provide minimal protection. If you, as most people, need death benefits, you are better off buying life insurance.

The truth is that death benefits sound much better than they play out. They come at a significant cost, and they provide minimal protection.

TRUTH 18

Annuities and income taxes

"The hardest thing in the world to understand is the income tax."

—Albert Einstein

One of the most confusing aspects of annuities is the income tax aspect of the investment. On one hand, proponents of annuities see the glass as half full and will tout the fact that annuities allow you to defer taxes for many years on the gains that you achieve through your annuity investment. Putting off paying income taxes until tomorrow or even the day after many tomorrows is very attractive to people who generally have a hate-hate relationship with the IRS.

However, people critical of annuities for income tax reasons will cite that when you do start paying income taxes on the money you receive from your annuity, the tax rate that you will pay will be at the much-dreaded ordinary income rates, which can be as high as 35%! They say that if you owned, outside of an annuity, the same mutual funds that make up the investment portion of your variable annuity, you would pay income taxes on your gains at lower capital gains rates, which are no greater than 15% and sometimes even as low as 5%. However, this is not as simple a comparison as it first appears.

So, let's look at the truth. No income taxes are due on your annuity's gains until you take money out of the annuity. While you are in what is referred to as the accumulation phase, your investment grows without your having to pay any income taxes on the gains that occur in the annuity. However, once you start taking money out of the annuity, Uncle Sam wants his share. The tax-deferral advantage of an annuity is of value to you only if you intend to hold your annuity as a long-term investment. The tax-deferral value is of little value to you if you need to access the money at a time when you will either be paying substantial surrender fees or receiving unfavorable IRS treatment for early withdrawals.

The tax-deferral advantage of an annuity is of value to you only if you intend to hold your annuity as a long-term investment.

A fixed annuity, where you receive a guaranteed rate of return, is often compared to an investment in a CD. Both are conservative investments. As with a CD, the longer you commit your money to the bank or insurance company, the higher the rate of return you are promised. Like a CD, when you take your money out of the annuity, a part of the payment you receive will be a return of the money you invested, which will not be taxed a second time. You were already taxed when you initially earned that money you used to purchase either the CD or the fixed annuity, and you did not get a tax deduction for the purchase of either the CD or the annuity. The amount that is exempt from income taxes in a fixed annuity is determined by a calculation of what is called the "exclusion ratio"—it is calculated by dividing the amount of your investment in the annuity by the total amount you receive in the particular payout period. However, what you receive as interest on the CD or gain on the fixed annuity are both subject to income taxation as ordinary income. It also should be noted, however, that if you are under the age of 59 1/2 and you choose to take your money out of a CD, there is no income tax penalty, whereas if you take your money out of a fixed annuity, you face a 10% income tax penalty.

However, when it comes to variable annuities, the comparison for income tax purposes is between the taxation of the mutual funds that form the investment accounts within your annuity with your owning pretty much the same mutual funds outside of your annuity. In this case, the income taxes will be significantly higher with the variable annuity. Calculating the specific tax ramifications of owning a variable annuity can be quite complicated. Unlike a fixed annuity, you do not know exactly what you will receive in the payments from your variable annuity. It is dependent upon how well your investments in the mutual fund-like sub-accounts that make up the investment portion of your annuity perform. The IRS determines the amount of the payment you receive that is tax-free by dividing the amount of your initial investment by your life expectancy in months. Therefore, if you invested $100,000 in an annuity and you have a life expectancy of 252 months (21 years), $396.82 of your monthly payment would be tax-free.

The IRS determines the amount of the payment you receive that is tax-free by dividing the amount of your initial investment by your life expectancy in months.

The preceding examples of payouts from fixed and variable annuities both share the premise that you are "annuitizing" your annuity, which means receiving a series of regular payments over a specific period of time or your lifetime. But what if you want to take money out of your annuity without annuitizing it? In this case, the IRS's rules are both simple and harsh. Since 1982, the IRS has taxed as ordinary income everything you take out until you have taken out all of the earnings over and above the amount that you have invested in the annuity. So, if you had an annuity that you purchased for $100,000 that is now worth $115,000, the first $15,000 you withdraw from the annuity will be considered income taxed as ordinary income. And, of course, the bad news does not end there. If you withdraw anything from your annuity prior to reaching the age of 59 ½, you will pay a 10% early withdrawal tax penalty.

A possibly significant tax benefit to a variable annuity when compared to a mutual fund is that investments in the mutual fund-like sub-accounts of an annuity can be changed regularly in an effort to balance the portfolio in regard to risk and suitability of the investments without incurring any income tax liability. The sale of mutual funds held by an investor outside of an annuity in an effort to achieve the same balanced portfolio would incur income taxes, albeit at the capital gains rate.

It should be noted that it is not just you, but also your heirs, who face the curse of the IRS. If you die owning a variable annuity, your heirs will pay ordinary income taxes on the gains of the annuity, whereas if you owned a mutual fund similar to the one that forms the investment portion of your annuity, your heirs would inherit the mutual fund with a step up in basis, which means that if they sold the mutual fund, they would pay income taxes only at capital gains rate and only on the increase in value of the mutual fund since your death.

TRUTH 19

Tax-free 1035 exchanges

"The pessimist sees difficulty in every opportunity. The optimist sees the opportunity in every difficulty."

—Winston Churchill

Not nearly as intriguing as Agent 007, but nowhere near as taxing as a Form 1040, is a tax-free 1035 exchange. The tax-free 1035 exchange gets its name from section 1035 of the Internal Revenue Code. Isn't it apt that the tax laws are referred to as being in code since sometimes it seems like you need a special decoder ring to be able to make sense of them? Fortunately, the tax-free 1035 exchange is not particularly complicated, but that does not mean that it is not fraught with potential problems.

At its essence, a tax-free 1035 exchange is the government's permission for you to be able to exchange one annuity contract for another annuity contract without being required to pay any income tax whatsoever on any gains in value of your original annuity. The switch from one annuity to another annuity does not even have to be with the same insurance company and is easy to accomplish. However, merely because it is easy to accomplish does not mean that you should do the exchange of annuities yourself. The dangers of not doing a tax-free 1035 exchange can be significant. Primary among the dangers is the rule that if you cash in your annuity and then take the money to purchase a new annuity, you will be subject to income taxes right away on the gains incurred in your previous annuity. The IRS is very much a stickler to their rule that in order to qualify as a tax-free 1035 exchange, you must never actually have access to the money from the first annuity. Rather, the IRS requires the insurance company that issued your initial annuity to cash out the annuity and send the money, not to you, but directly to the new insurance company that is issuing you your new annuity.

The IRS is very much a stickler to their rule that in order to qualify as a tax-free 1035 exchange, you must never actually have access to the money from the first annuity.

The better option by far if you wish to do a tax-free 1035 exchange of one annuity for another annuity is to merely fill out a 1035 exchange request form and provide it to the new insurance company along with your application for the new annuity. They will be more than happy (I always wondered what "more than happy" means, but I am still afraid to ask) to do the work for you because they stand to profit handsomely from your purchase of a new annuity from them. You are also required to provide the insurance company with your original annuity contract; however, if like many people, you cannot locate it, all you have to do is fill out a lost contract form and provide this to the new insurance company, which will do all of the heavy lifting.

There is no limit to the number of times a year that you may do a tax-free 1035 exchange. You may do as many tax-free 1035 exchanges as you have annuity contracts. In fact, the IRS even allows you to exchange a portion of the value of an existing annuity contract for another annuity without any income taxes being incurred. However, the insurance company that issued your original policy may not be so similarly inclined, and if the terms of your initial annuity contract do not, in fact, allow a partial exchange, this option will not be available to you regardless of what the tax law states.

But why would you want to exchange an annuity in the first place?

You may have been convinced by a salesperson, or even by your own research, that the terms of a new annuity are much more advantageous to you than the terms found in your original annuity. The new annuity may provide you with more and better investment alternatives for the sub-accounts that make up the annuity. Or, perhaps, there is a more advantageous death benefit (although that is an oxymoron if I ever heard one). Whatever your reason for considering switching, you should always be cognizant of the fact that there is a long and dark history of unethical financial advisors convincing people to switch annuities to ones that they are selling, not because ultimately they provide a better investment for the customer, but because they provide greater commissions to the financial advisor. Most financial advisors are knowledgeable, hard-working people, but a slick, unethical financial advisor can do more harm to your financial well-being with a pen than any thief with a gun could do. And I hate to even contemplate what an unethical financial advisor could do with both a gun and a pen.

So, what should you be on the look-out for?

You should make sure that you understand what surrender penalties are in effect if you exchange your present annuity for a new annuity.

First and foremost, you should make sure that you understand what surrender penalties are in effect if you exchange your present annuity for a new annuity. Although the exchange of your old annuity for a new annuity may indeed be a tax-free exchange, and your new annuity may provide enhanced value when compared to your present annuity, the surrender penalties of your old policy may ultimately make the tax-free 1035 annuity exchange a bad choice for you. With annuity surrender fees and penalties continuing for as many as ten years or even longer, they just may make any tax-free 1035 annuity exchange too costly for you. Even if you are out of the surrender period for your old annuity (so that you could exchange the annuity for another annuity without a surrender fee having to be paid to the insurance company that issued your original annuity), you may wish to take a moment to consider the fact that when you start over with a new annuity, you most likely are also starting over with a new penalty period that limits your options in regard to getting at your money early without substantial penalties.

Finally, whenever you are comparing annuities, make sure you fully understand not just what the annuity appears to be offering you by way of features, but also what the cost of those various features will be. Read the prospectus. I know it is not light reading, but it is the only place that you have a chance of truly learning what is the real cost of the new annuity. Because some fees are not apparent other than in the prospectus, you owe it to yourself to make sure that you understand what you actually will be getting for your money and how much you will have to spend to get the new bells and whistles that initially attracted you to the new annuity.

TRUTH 20

Charitable gift annuities

"If I am not for myself, who will be for me? If I am not for others, what am I? And if not now, when?"

—Rabbi Hillel

Philanthropically inclined people looking for the guaranteed lifetime income of an annuity might well consider a charitable gift annuity. Many charities, such as the Red Cross or the Salvation Army, prominently feature charitable gift annuities as a major fund-raising activity that is seen by them as presenting a win-win situation whereby the individual gets income for life while the charity ultimately is the beneficiary of a substantial charitable gift.

Instead of purchasing an annuity from an insurance company, with a charitable gift annuity you buy the annuity directly from the charity. The charity agrees to pay you and, if you wish, your spouse, an income for life. When you die, any remaining value in the annuity is paid to the charity. If you buy the annuity and live beyond your actuarially determined lifetime, you come out ahead. The charity is still bound to pay you for as long as you live. If you die before your actuarially determined life expectancy, you lose money on the amount you paid as compared to what you received from the charity through annuity payments, while the charity gets a larger gift. Complicating things further, a charitable gift annuity is irrevocable. Once you buy it, you cannot cash it in.

Also, in the good news-bad news category, your payments will always remain the same. This is good news because you have a steady, guaranteed income for life. This is bad news because the income you receive from the annuity payments will not keep pace with inflation.

A charitable gift annuity is irrevocable. Once you buy it, you cannot cash it in.

Speaking of the guaranteed income, any guaranteed charitable gift annuity is only as good as the charity from which you purchase it. Therefore, it makes much sense for you to consider buying a charitable gift annuity only from well-established, financially solid charities. Fortunately, it is not difficult to obtain financial information on the financial status of various charities. The American Institute of Philanthropy (www.charitywatch.org) is just one of a number of organizations that can provide you with information as to the financial strength and security of particular charities from which you may be considering buying a charitable gift annuity. In addition, the individual states have their own requirements as to the amount of money that must be set aside by charities in annuity reserve funds.

The amount of money that you receive from the charity through a charitable gift annuity is dependent upon a number of factors, including your age, whether the annuity will be for yourself alone or with a spouse or other person, the amount that you give to the charity, and the interest rate that the charity sets at the time that you purchase the annuity. A common annuity payment rate for a single person aged 60 is 5.7%, and for a joint and survivor annuity where both people are 60 years old, a common annuity payment rate is 5.4%. If, however, you wait until both you and your spouse are at least 95 years old, the good news is that most charities will generously pay you an annual rate of return of 11.1%. The bad news, however, is that they pay this high rate of return because they do not expect you to return to them for many payments. The interest rate that you receive from a charitable gift annuity most likely will be somewhat less than what you could receive from a comparable annuity issued by an insurance company; however, this is offset by the additional tax benefits that you receive for the charitable donation aspect of the charitable gift annuity purchase and, of course, by the satisfaction of making a contribution to a charity near and dear to your heart.

Tax laws are written not just to take your money, but also to encourage certain activities and discourage others. When you buy a charitable gift annuity, you receive an immediate tax deduction based upon the amount of the value of your annuity that IRS actuaries estimate will be left to the charity at your death. For example, if a 67-year-old man paid $50,000 for a charitable gift annuity, he would get an immediate tax deduction in the amount of $19,843 as a charitable deduction that he could use to lower his present income tax liability.

When you buy a charitable gift annuity, you receive an immediate tax deduction based upon the amount of the value of your annuity that IRS actuaries estimate will be left to the charity at your death.

You also get another tax break, as you do with other annuities, whereby a portion of your monthly payment comes back to you untaxed as a return of your purchase price while the remainder of the money paid to you is taxed at ordinary income rates. So for example, if a 65-year-old bought a charitable gift annuity for himself or herself alone, of the $3,000 annual payment he or she would receive, only $1,380 of it would be subject to income tax.

Sometimes you can achieve additional tax benefits by donating to charity stocks, bonds, or real estate that had a low tax basis such that were you to sell them, you would be subject to a significant capital gains income tax liability. However, by passing these assets to the charity, you are able to avoid the income tax and put more of the value of those assets to work for you in the charitable gift annuity that the charity gives you in return for your donation of the low basis-high value property. Meanwhile, because charities are tax-exempt organizations, it is able to sell the assets given to it without having to incur any income tax. So everyone wins.

As with commercial annuities issued by insurance companies, you can choose to have your charitable gift annuity provide for immediate or deferred payments. The most commonly chosen form of payment is an immediate payment that is made four times per year. However, you can choose to have your payments deferred to a date of your choosing at least a year after the date of the purchase of the annuity. In fact, you can even make the decision as to when you will commence annuity payments after you buy the annuity. You pick an initial deferred starting date for your annuity payments, but keep the flexibility of being able to change that starting date. The longer you put off starting your annuity payments, the larger your annual payments would be.

TRUTH 21

Split annuities

"In investing money, the amount of interest you want should depend on whether you want to eat well or sleep well."

—Kenfield Morley

Split annuities are the surf and turf of annuities. Just as when you go to a restaurant and can't quite decide which is best, the steak or the fish, so you get a dinner that consists of both, so it is with split annuities—except in this case, there is nothing fishy about your choice. You don't need to decide whether to pick the immediate annuity and its guaranteed payment of income or a deferred annuity with its promise of greater, tax-deferred returns later down the road. With split annuities, you can have both.

The split in split annuities refers to taking the money that you consider investing in annuities and dividing the money between two separate annuities. The first annuity is a single premium immediate annuity that will provide you with a guaranteed stream of income for the fixed period of your choice that can be anywhere up to twenty years, but is commonly for a lesser period, such as five years. The amount that you receive each month from your single premium immediate annuity is based upon a number of factors, including the current interest rates at the time that you initiate the contract and the time period during which you will receive payments. Although you can choose to make the single premium immediate annuity portion of the split annuity a variable annuity in order to enhance the potential for receiving more benefit from the annuity, many people utilizing the split annuity strategy choose fixed annuities so that they have the security of knowing what their regular monthly payment will be. However, there is nothing preventing you from having multiple annuities for the immediate portion of your split annuity strategy and using both a fixed annuity and a variable annuity to provide you with the income to meet your present expenses.

Deep in the heart of taxes

When you purchase your immediate annuity with after-tax funds, the payments to you from the immediate annuity that commence immediately are only partially subject to income taxes. As with all payments from annuities, you pay income taxes on the earnings of your annuity at ordinary income tax rates and not at lower capital gains rates. However, with an immediate annuity, a significant amount of your regular monthly payments are characterized by the

Internal Revenue Service as a return of your initial investment in the annuity and therefore are not taxable.

Single premium deferred annuity

The second component of the split annuity strategy is a single premium deferred annuity that you purchase at the same time that you buy the immediate annuity. The single premium immediate annuity provides instant gratification and an income to help meet your financial needs today, whereas the single premium deferred annuity is the money that you are investing for your needs some years down the road. Like other deferred annuities, your money grows tax-deferred in the annuity. This not only permits you to avoid income taxes until you take out the money at the maturity of the annuity, but it also lets the money invested in the deferred annuity compound, at the potentially higher rates possible with a variable annuity.

Maturity

For many baby boomers, maturity has always been a dirty word and a condition we have consistently avoided. However, with the split annuity strategy, maturity is just one part of the strategy. When the immediate annuity has been exhausted after whatever payout period you have chosen, you are then faced with the decision as to what to do with your single premium deferred annuity. You have the choice of taking the payments for whatever payout period you picked for your single premium deferred annuity, which can be either a period-certain, life only, life and period-certain, joint and survivor, or whatever other option you have chosen. However, you also

The single premium immediate annuity provides instant gratification and an income to help meet your financial needs today, whereas the single premium deferred annuity is the money that you are investing for your needs some years down the road.

have another option. You can choose to start the whole process over again by taking your money from the deferred annuity and investing a portion of it in an immediate annuity to take advantage of whatever the present interest rates may be at that time and putting the rest of it into another deferred annuity. Generally, insurance companies will sell annuities to anyone up to the age of 85.

For many people, this strategy is a safe way of staying current with interest rate fluctuations and making their retirement investment dollars work longer for them. Thus, you can get the best of both worlds: steady retirement income for today and growth for future retirement needs.

Disclaimer: This strategy can work well for people who do not require the full income of their initial investment amount that is divided between the two annuities in order to meet their present income needs. However, with that bit of a disclaimer, this can be an effective strategy to keep your money working for you as long as possible.

Shop around

Although the split annuity strategy is a unified annuity purchasing strategy, it is neither required nor necessarily advantageous for you to buy both the immediate and the deferred annuities that make up the strategy from the same company. As Yoda advised Luke Skywalker, "Use the force." Except here you should use the force of your dollars and go to whatever companies are offering the best deals for the individual annuities that you need to make the strategy work.

As always, it is not what you make that is important—it is what you keep that counts. Fees always chip away at your earnings. Choose annuities from safe, strong companies with the lowest fees. The company that may offer you the best deal for your immediate annuity may not be the company that offers you the best deal for your deferred annuity. There is nothing improper, illegal, immoral, unethical, or fattening about buying the two annuities that you need to make this strategy work from different companies. In addition, buying the annuities from different companies spreads your risk.

TRUTH 22

Joint and survivor annuities

"You can be young without money, but you can't be old without it."

—Tennessee Williams

"Stay out of expensive joints" was the advice that I received in law school from one of my professors. He was referring to the potential financial risks of jointly owned property and perhaps even expensive restaurants, but he also could have been talking about joint and survivor annuities.

When a married person buys an annuity, he or she has a number of different settlement options from which he or she may choose. Although the highest monthly payout will be received through a settlement option that provides for payments to continue only for the life of the person purchasing the annuity, married people are rightfully concerned about what happens if they predecease their spouses. Will the surviving spouse have enough money to live on? Buying an annuity that will pay a steady income to both spouses throughout their lifetimes regardless of who dies first is attractive, but will reduce the amount of the monthly payment significantly. However, there are other choices. The insurance companies provide a number of different settlement options from which a married couple may choose in an effort to find the right annuity for their particular situation and risk tolerance.

Some of the settlement options include the following:

1. Joint and survivor payout (100%). Through this choice, the surviving spouse will continue to receive the same benefits as was received while both were alive, for the rest of her life.
2. Joint and survivor (50%) first or either. Through this choice, the surviving spouse will continue to receive payments after the death of one of them; however, the payments will be reduced by 50%. A variation of this choice to provide for payments of 75% of the previous payments to the surviving spouse is also available. Payments from either of these settlement options will be higher than those they would have received had they chosen the joint and survivor payout of 100%.
3. Joint and survivor (50%) only primary annuitant. In this choice, instead of co-annuitants, the annuity-buying spouse will not have his annuity payments reduced if his spouse dies. If, however, he predeceases his wife, the payments to the wife would be reduced by half. Again, another variation of this option provides for payments of 75% of the previous

payments upon the death of the annuity owner. This is a choice to consider if the annuity-owning spouse has a spouse who is not in very good health.

There are many more joint and survivor settlement options, including some with guaranteed payments for specific periods of time and others with provisions for return of premium.

The main issue facing a married couple deciding what settlement option to take is that the greater the percentage of the annuity payment that they pick for the surviving spouse to receive, the less they both will receive while both of them are alive.

But there is another choice. Instead of looking to the annuity to be the primary source of retirement funds following the death of the first spouse to die, they may instead choose to take the higher annuity settlement payout option for the lifetime of the annuity-purchasing spouse only. They could then use some of that additional money they receive from this higher payment to purchase life insurance that would be available at the time of the death of the annuity-purchasing spouse to replace the money lost at the annuity's termination.

For example, a healthy 65-year-old man paying $100,000 for an immediate annuity in Massachusetts with payments to be made only for his lifetime, with no payments to a surviving spouse or anyone else, would receive payments of $672 per month for the rest of his life. If he had chosen a joint and survivor settlement option that would have paid his surviving spouse the full amount of the regular monthly payments for the rest of her life, the amount received would be reduced to $577 per month. If he took the higher monthly payout for the annuity that would pay only during his lifetime, he could take some of the extra money provided by this higher payout to purchase life insurance to meet the needs of his wife upon his death if he should predecease her and the annuity payments terminate.

Using this strategy of taking the higher annuity payout that terminates upon the death of the spouse buying the annuity also has the advantage of potentially providing for a legacy through the life insurance to pass on to the couple's children in the event that the surviving spouse does not use the full amount of the life insurance during her lifetime, or if the spouse not buying the annuity should predecease her husband. In either event, the life insurance proceeds would be available for the couple's children. If a joint and survivor annuity option had been chosen, there would be nothing left to pass on to the children following the deaths of their parents. Of course, an essential element of this strategy is that the person buying the annuity payable only for his lifetime would also have to be able to obtain a life insurance policy at a reasonable rate. Whether a person is able to get a life insurance policy, and the premiums that he will be required to pay for the policy, is dependent upon his health at the time he applies for the life insurance policy, so this strategy is only useful to older people in good health.

This strategy can be very useful if both the husband and wife are about the same age and equally healthy. If the wife is substantially younger than her husband, in better health, and could be expected to live as long as 15 more years than the husband, the joint and survivor settlement option is probably the better choice. However, for many retirees who are married to someone close to their own age and are in a similar state of health, the higher-paying annuity settlement option coupled with life insurance may be a great choice.

For many retirees who are married to someone close to their own age and are in a similar state of health, the higher-paying annuity settlement option coupled with life insurance may be a great choice.

Before making this decision, you should therefore consider the following items:

1. How old is each person?
2. What are their relative life expectancies?
3. What are their relative states of health?
4. What will be the cost of insurance?
5. What is the difference in payments received in the annuity from a lifetime only payout and a joint and survivor payout?

TRUTH 23

Shorter surrender annuities

"In theory, there is no difference between theory and practice. In practice there is."

—Yogi Berra

One of the greatest drawbacks to the purchase of any annuity is the surrender fee. Most annuities have surrender fees that can extend anywhere from seven to ten years or more. If you need to have access to the money that you invested in the annuity during the surrender period, you pay a significant penalty fee that can drastically eat into the value of your investment.

Generally, the surrender fee is a percentage of the money that you withdraw over and above any amount that you are permitted to withdraw without a penalty. Usually, the amount that you can withdraw penalty-free is 10% of the value of your annuity; but if you need to get at more than that for whatever reason, be it adverse health issues or just because you need the money for your ordinary living expenses, you are assessed a penalty that can be as much as 7% or more. Most often the penalty fee goes down by a percent each year that you own the annuity, but it still presents a significant impediment to your access to your money. It is for this reason that deferred annuities are considered not to be an appropriate investment for many older people who may either expect to need access to their money in the next few years or are at a substantial risk of having events occur that would require them to get at the money in the annuity.

Usually, the amount that you can withdraw penalty-free is 10% of the value of your annuity.

For many reasons, but particularly the surrender fee, deferred annuities should always be bought with the understanding that they are a long-term investment. This is not to say that the insurance companies are bad people by having surrender fees. Although surrender fees can be exorbitant and have a harmful effect on the value of your annuity, there is a rationale for them. If the insurance company is going to guarantee a certain interest rate on the annuities that it issues, it has to be able to count on having the money at its disposal to invest in longer-term investments to generate the money necessary to meet their obligations to their annuity holders. Of course, that does not make the surrender fee any easier to take when you need to get money out of your annuity. And to make things even worse, if you withdraw money from your annuity during the surrender period before you reach the magic age of 59½, you not only will have to pay a surrender fee on any amounts you take out greater than 10% of the value of your annuity, but also a federal excise tax of 10% on the money you withdraw as well. For example, if at age 58, you had a $100,000 annuity, and you withdrew $20,000 from the annuity in the first year of the annuity at a time when the surrender fee was 7%, you would have to pay a $2,000 federal excise tax. Then, to add insult to injury, you would also have to pay an additional $700 as a surrender fee. A pretty high price to pay just to get your own money back.

But now to your rescue come the insurance companies.

For the insurance companies, everything is an opportunity to sell you another product. Annuities come with an almost endless, complicated variety of provisions. If you are looking at the glass as half-full, you would say that the insurance companies are tailoring their products to your own particular needs, and to some extent this is true. However, if you are one of those people who look at the glass and not only see it as half-empty, but also just a little bit dirty and maybe even cracked, you might see the variations of the basic annuity as just another way to charge new fees that provide benefits that may be more illusory than real.

In response to people being upset with annuities with long surrender periods, the insurance companies have come up with a new breed of annuity called "L Share Variable Annuities." These annuities have significantly shorter surrender periods of as little as three years. What a deal!

You might see the variations of the basic annuity as just another way to charge new fees that provide benefits that may be more illusory than real.

But is it?

The truth is that the insurance companies giveth and the insurance companies taketh away. On one hand, you get an annuity with a surrender period of half of what you would have in a more traditional annuity, but you also get a Mortality and Expense Administration

Fee that is significantly larger than what you would find in a more traditional annuity. So you are paying for this lower surrender fee in spades. But wait.... It doesn't end there. In addition to the higher Morality and Expense Administration Fee, you also may have higher surrender fees in the three or four years that a surrender fee applies in this new annuity. Certainly you shouldn't buy any annuity if there is the distinct possibility that you will need to get at the money in the short run, but sometimes you cannot anticipate when you will need access to the money in your annuity. With one of these new lower surrender period L Share Variable Annuities, you actually could end up paying more if you need to get at your money in the first few years of the annuity than if you had a longer surrender period annuity through a combination of higher surrender fees and a higher Mortality and Expense Administration Fee.

In addition to the L Share Variable Annuities with shorter surrender periods, insurance companies are now also offering C Share Variable Annuities that have no surrender charges whatsoever. However, the fees that you pay for this provision outweigh any benefit you might have by eliminating the surrender charge. And of course, you are still subject to the early withdrawal tax penalties if you take money out of your annuity before age 59 ½.

So are there any good reasons for buying a lower surrender annuity?

There may be. If you are buying one as a long-term investment, but with the intention to have the flexibility of being able to exchange it after a few years for the next generation of annuities through a tax-free 1035 exchange, it may make sense to consider a lower surrender period annuity. Annuities are constantly changing, and although the essential elements of annuities remain the same, the competition among issuers of annuities to come up with annuities that are more attractive to investors continues to bring us annuities with more favorable terms, and in even some instances, fewer fees.

TRUTH 24

Longevity insurance

"I intend to live forever, or die trying."

—Groucho Marx

The good news is that people are living longer today than ever before. The bad news is that many people are fearful that a lifetime's savings won't provide enough money for a lifetime. At one time, it was common for many people, at retirement, to put their money almost exclusively in fixed income instruments such as Certificates of Deposit. But all of that has changed. The truth is that the steady income provided by CDs is not much more than a recipe for slowly going broke as inflation eats into your returns.

Everything is an opportunity for someone. And for the insurance companies, the combination of a longer living population with the fear that the sources of income with which they are comfortable will not be enough spawned the recent development of what is commonly known as longevity insurance.

Longevity insurance is just another form of annuity. You pay the insurance company a lump sum of money, and they pay you a steady, fixed payment for life. The special twist with longevity insurance is that although you may purchase the policy at age 65, for example, the policy will not start to pay you until you reach the age of 85. In essence, longevity insurance is just a variation on a deferred fixed annuity with a fancier name. However, there are some key differences. A typical deferred fixed annuity involves your paying the insurance company a lump sum and after a period of time—for example, 20 years—you start receiving fixed, regular payments for the rest of your life. But the money that you receive will be less than that typically paid by a longevity insurance annuity. Considerably less. A typical $10,000 fixed deferred annuity bought at age 65 that starts paying at age 85 would pay $137 per month. But a typical longevity insurance annuity bought at age 65 that began paying at age 85 would pay $710 per month—a considerable difference. The reason for that

The special twist with longevity insurance is that although you may purchase the policy at age 65, for example, the policy will not start to pay you until you reach the age of 85.

great discrepancy in payments can be found in the fine print of your policy. A typical fixed deferred annuity will permit you to withdraw the money before the deferral period is up and will also generally have a death benefit. By eliminating these provisions, the insurance company is able to project that it will not make as many payments under the terms of longevity insurance annuities and therefore can afford to offer a larger payout. In essence, the insurance companies are betting that they will be making payments to fewer policy holders and therefore can afford to pay more to those who do reach the policy-paying age of 85.

Bells and whistles

As with just about any annuity, there are a number of bells and whistles that you can add to the basic longevity insurance annuity policy to tailor it more to your needs. Inflation protection is a critical add-on to any policy because the value of a payout 20 years later is sure to be diluted by inflation. A death benefit can also be added to the policy, making it more like the traditional fixed, deferred annuity. A withdrawal option also similar to the traditional fixed, deferred annuity can also be added to your policy. Another particularly interesting add-on is a provision for early payments restricted to use for nursing home costs. This can be particularly attractive to someone who wishes to obtain some sort of coverage for long-term care in a nursing home, but is unable to obtain conventional long-term care insurance for medical reasons. It is important to remember, however, that the louder the bells and whistles, the greater the costs. Every one of these add-ons also brings considerable cost to the annuity, which reduces the benefit of the longevity insurance annuity.

Alternative investment strategy

It was that great investment strategist, Dirty Harry, who reduced the investment strategy of many people to its essence when he said, "Do you feel lucky?" Actually, he also added, " Do you, punk?," but I think that is a bit too harsh for our purposes. The fact of the matter is that many people invest conservatively because they may believe that investing in the stock market is particularly risky and that luck plays a large part in it. But what if you knew you had a steady, guaranteed source of income to meet a portion of your needs in the future? Would you feel more comfortable taking greater risks with the rest of your investment portfolio, knowing that even if you were not lucky, a good portion of your financial needs would be met by other investments? Would you feel more comfortable swinging for the fences, knowing you already had a four-run lead? That is the opportunity that longevity insurance annuities present you. By guaranteeing that you will have a portion of your needs met in the future, you are able to take greater risks with the remainder of your investment portfolio and put yourself in a position to reap greater rewards, secure in the knowledge that your longevity insurance annuity will be around to meet a portion of your needs in your final years.

A few rules of thumb

If you subscribe to the old rock-and-roll mantra of "live hard, die young, and leave a good-looking corpse," a longevity insurance annuity is not for you. On the other hand, if your family has longevity and you expect to live well into your 80s and beyond, you may wish to consider this product.

Longevity insurance annuities represent a long-term relationship with the insurance company from which you purchase the policy. Don't be penny-wise and pound-foolish by purchasing a policy at a low premium from a company that is not financially stable. Be confident that the company with which you are dealing is likely to be around in the future.

If your family has longevity and you expect to live well into your 80s and beyond, you may wish to consider this product.

The older you are, the more likely you will get a better payout from a traditional deferred annuity, so if you are not expecting to buy an annuity until you are in your 70s, you are better off passing on the longevity insurance annuity.

TRUTH 25

Inheriting an annuity

"A very rich person should leave his kids enough to do anything, but not enough to do nothing."

—Warren Buffet

Although people buy annuities to provide a safe and secure income stream in retirement, many people end up dying without ever drinking from that stream. Some people are just frugal and find that they do not need the money contained in their annuity. They leave it untapped within the annuity to continue to grow on a tax-deferred basis for their children. Others find themselves looking at their annuities as half-empty glasses and obsess about the large income tax hit they will take when they withdraw money from the annuity and confront their day of reckoning with the IRS.

If the owner of an annuity dies after the annuity has already started to pay regular payments (annuitization), the payments will continue depending on the particular settlement option chosen. (See Truth 14, "Annuity Settlement Options.") However, if the settlement option chosen was a lifetime-only payout, all bets are off, and the payments terminate with nothing being paid further from the annuity to a surviving spouse or any other designated beneficiary. This is the price you pay for choosing that particular payout option.

If the lifetime-only payout was not chosen and a surviving spouse is the designated beneficiary of the annuity, the surviving spouse generally has the option to become the new owner of the annuity and continue the contract, as well as continue the tax deferral if she chooses. In fact, if that surviving spouse remarries and names the new spouse as a beneficiary, the tax deferral can be extended until both of them have died.

If the owner of an annuity dies after the annuity has already started to pay regular payments (annuitization), the payments will continue depending on the particular settlement option chosen.

Ultimately, however, you run out of spouses, the piper (not to mention the IRS) must be paid, and the money taken out of the annuity. When the annuity owner dies and there is no surviving spouse, the beneficiaries, who often are the children of the annuity owner, have essentially four options as to how they will take the money in the annuity. Each of these options has distinct income tax ramifications.

Option 1—Take the money from the annuity in a lump sum and pay the income taxes on the gains accrued in the annuity at ordinary income tax rates. This option presents a potentially large income tax bill in one year and may result in putting the beneficiary in a higher income tax bracket, resulting in even more income taxes owed.

Option 2—Take distributions in such amounts as the beneficiary shall determine over the next five years. This option gives the beneficiary some level of control over the amount of income taxes paid by giving the beneficiary the power to decide the amounts of income taken in any of the five years.

Option 3—Wait and continue the tax deferral for five full years and then take full payment of the annuity, at which time an even larger tax bill will be owed than at the death of the annuity owner because the annuity continued to grow tax-deferred during those years. To put this option in the most favorable light, however, although there would be a larger tax bill at the end of the five years, there also would be the benefits of an additional five years of compounded, tax-deferred gains.

Option 4—If the original annuity owner had taken a lifetime payout with period certain, he can continue the payments over the remaining period certain, which may be five, ten, fifteen, or twenty years. (See Truth 14 for more details on this.) This option must be exercised within one year of the death of the original annuity owner and serves to spread out both the income taxes as well as future tax-deferral over the remaining years of the term certain at the death of the original owner of the annuity.

On top of any income taxes that will be owed pertaining to payments from the annuity, the full value of the annuity is included in the estate of the original owner of the annuity for estate tax purposes. So if the estate is subject to estate taxes, an annuity may present a double tax whammy.

Substituting a life insurance policy for an annuity

Depending on who owns the policy, life insurance proceeds are subject to estate tax and are not subject to income tax, which is a significant financial benefit of life insurance. Life insurance is an effective way to pass on wealth to the next generation. But how do you take the money out of an annuity and put it into a life insurance policy? Unfortunately, the answer is that there is no way to do so without paying income taxes when you cash in the annuity. However, this may be one time that it makes sense to cash in the annuity, pay your income tax, and get the money working for you as soon as possible in a life insurance policy. Even after paying the income taxes due upon cashing in an annuity, using those after-tax proceeds to purchase a life insurance will end up providing significantly more to beneficiaries who ultimately are paid the proceeds of the life insurance policy free of income tax rather than having them inherit the annuity and all of the income taxes that come with it. In addition, if the owner of the annuity cashes it in and replaces it with a life insurance policy, he will have the cash value of that policy at his disposal if he needs that money during his lifetime.

TIP Another interesting way of coupling life insurance and annuities to benefit heirs is through the purchase of an immediate annuity with a single lump-sum payment. The annuity must provide for immediate payout over a period of at least five years. This money received from the annuity can then, in turn, be used to purchase a whole life insurance policy, one with a cash value. The owner of the policy then can borrow money from the insurance policy for his income needs so long as he keeps the policy in effect and does not borrow all the cash value of the policy. Then, at the death of the insured, the substantial death benefit passes to the beneficiaries of the policy without having to pay any income taxes.

TRUTH 26

Variable annuities versus variable universal life insurance

"Dealing with complexity is an inefficient and unnecessary waste of time, attention, and mental energy. There is never any justification for things being complex when they could be simple."

—Edward de Bono

For those of you who just can't live your lives without considering every possible way of achieving your goal, we have this interesting comparison between complex variable annuities and equally as complex variable universal life insurance policies as vehicles for retirement savings.

Variable universal life insurance

This is a relatively new creature in the evolution of insurance policies. It combines parts of universal life insurance policies with parts of variable life insurance policies to come up with a new type of life insurance policy that combines term life insurance, with its attendant lower premiums, with the ability to invest part of the premiums in mutual fund-like sub-accounts similar to those found in variable life insurance policies.

Similar to a variable annuity, you are able to achieve a tax-deferred increase in value of the sub-accounts. Unlike a variable annuity that will subject you to income taxes on your withdrawals at high ordinary income tax rates, money you take out of your variable universal life insurance policy can be done through a low interest loan from your own policy without incurring any income taxes whatsoever. In addition, you have the added benefit of the life insurance coverage to be able to pass on to your heirs.

So, it looks like a good deal. But is it?

The truth is that this is a complicated investment choice. First, because a part of the premium from your variable universal life insurance policy is applied toward the cost of maintaining the life insurance coverage within the policy, not all of your premium money is working for you in your sub-accounts, although this negative aspect of the variable universal life insurance policy must be balanced against the fact that ultimately you will be paying both

Money you take out of your variable universal life insurance policy can be done through a low interest loan from your own policy without incurring any income taxes.

federal and state income taxes on money that you would take out of your variable annuity. As always, it is necessary to do your homework and crunch your numbers.

In addition, a variable universal life insurance policy is fraught with fees that, once again, prompt us to consider our mantra, "It is not what you make, but what you keep, that is important." The portion of your premium that goes to cover the cost of the term life insurance portion of your policy is, more likely, to be greater than the cost of a corresponding amount of term life insurance had you bought it outside of your variable universal life insurance policy. Then there are the investment management fees, the mortality and expense charges (M&E), as well as a host of other fees that may appear within your policy and reduce the bang for your bucks. In this respect, a universal variable life insurance policy is starting to resemble a typical variable annuity with its own potentially long list of fees, including its own investment management fees and M&E charges. Once again, it is necessary for you to shop around, do your homework, and compare the actual costs of variable universal life insurance policies and variable annuities that you may be considering.

So, what about your tax-free loan withdrawals from a variable universal life insurance policy?

Variable universal life insurance policies are like luggage and herpes—once you get them, you have them for the rest of your life. If you permit the variable universal life insurance policy to lapse, all of the investment earnings that you have borrowed from the sub-accounts become taxable. If you have been borrowing tax-free from the variable universal life insurance policy throughout your retirement and suddenly find that it is necessary to permit the policy to lapse, you will be stuck with a significant tax bill on all of the earnings you have borrowed from your policy.

If you permit the variable universal life insurance policy to lapse, all of the investment earnings that you have borrowed from the sub-accounts become taxable.

Life insurance policies should not be bought unless you need life insurance, and a variable universal life insurance policy is no exception to this rule. The fees that you incur and the lack of flexibility of the policy make this an investment that should not be considered unless you have both a need for life insurance (that you can purchase more cost-effectively with another type of policy) and have already put as much money as you can into other more effective and, dare I say it, simpler tax-deferred investments.

In addition, as with variable annuities, there are applicable surrender fees that can eat into the value, as well as the flexibility of owning a variable universal life insurance policy. Of course, rather than let the policy lapse, you always can consider converting the policy to another type of insurance policy.

The bottom line is that comparing variable universal life insurance policies and variable annuities is comparing two types of complex investments, where the best choice may well be to choose neither of them. In any event, the choice itself is one that requires a great deal of research and careful evaluation.

The bottom line is that comparing variable universal life insurance policies and variable annuities is comparing two types of complex investments, where the best choice may well be to choose neither of them.

TRUTH 27

Choosing between mutual funds and an annuity

"It's not whether you win or lose, it's how you play the game."

—Grantland Rice

It is not how you play the game that is important; it is whether you win or lose—at least when it comes to retirement investing. So, where will you score better: in a variable annuity or by owning mutual funds outside of an annuity?

Figures lie and liars figure. You will find plenty of people with complicated sets of figures to support their proposition that variable annuities are a better investment than owning mutual funds. These people generally are looking to sell you a variable annuity.

But they are wrong. Their figures are fatally flawed and based upon erroneous assumptions. The truth is that you are better off investing in mutual funds than in a variable annuity.

So let's compare.

One of the biggest lies is that when you invest in a variable annuity, 100% of your money is working for you. You are told that you pay no commissions. That is accurate. It is also misleading. Although you may not be paying a commission, designated as such, out of your pocket, do you really think you are getting this investment for free? You pay the commission through the fees that proliferate throughout variable annuities. Buried within the fine print of variable annuities is a trail of fees that eat into your profits. You will also pay to invest in a mutual fund. In fact, some of the fees that you may pay in some mutual funds are every bit as outrageous as those found in some variable annuities. However, you also have the option to invest in a tax-advantaged index mutual fund with extremely low fees unrivaled by any other comparable investment, so that ultimately more of your money is working for you in a tax-advantaged index mutual fund than in a variable annuity.

You will find plenty of people with complicated sets of figures to support their proposition that variable annuities are a better investment than owning mutual funds. These people generally are looking to sell you a variable annuity.

There is no question that investing in a variable annuity will permit you to not only invest in mutual fund-like sub-accounts in your annuity, but also provide you with entrance into the wonderful world of tax deferral. Compounding the gains on a tax-deferred investment is admittedly a strong selling point for a variable annuity. Unfortunately, it is more than compensated for by the fact that when the gains ultimately come out of your annuity, they will be taxed at high ordinary income tax rates rather than low capital gains rates if you had invested in a mutual fund outside of an annuity.

When you do take money out of a mutual fund, you will be taxed on your gains at lower capital gains rates. The gains in your mutual fund also are not subject to the slings and arrows of outrageous surrender charges and penalties for early withdrawals, as well as federal income tax penalties if you need to take out the money before the magic age of 59 ½. A mutual fund not only earns you more money, but also provides you with greater flexibility and access to your money without financial penalties.

And what if you should die while owning a variable annuity as compared to dying while owning a tax-advantaged index mutual fund? If your children inherit your variable annuity, they will be subject to income tax on the entire gain in the variable annuity at ordinary tax rates. This represents a large potential tax hit for them. However, if they were to inherit the same money that had been invested in a tax-advantaged mutual fund, they would receive a step-up in basis as to the mutual fund. So, not only would they be taxed at lower capital gains rates on the gains in the mutual fund they inherit, but because their basis would be the value of the mutual fund at the time of the death of their parent, if they sold the mutual fund shortly after inheriting it, they would owe absolutely no income tax at all—in the eyes of the IRS, they would have no taxable gain. Contrast this to ordinary income tax rates as high as 35% for the inheriting children on the gains in a variable annuity, and you have another significant advantage to owning tax-advantaged mutual funds as compared to owning a variable annuity.

Fans of variable annuities will also tell you that they provide a guarantee as to the safety of your money invested that you just cannot get in any mutual fund. They are right. But with a long-term investment, such as an annuity, how valuable is this guarantee?

Historically, the value is little because over time, the market always recovers. Did you possibly think that this guarantee came without cost? Of course not. You pay for a guarantee of little value with fees that further reduce your gains.

Just as the annuity industry is constantly evolving and developing new variations to better meet people's needs, so is the mutual fund industry, which is fully aware of the investing public's desire for a product that provides a safe and steady stream of income like an annuity, without all of the fees and limitations of an annuity. In October 2007, Schwab started the first of what will probably be many mutual funds aimed at providing such a steady income source coupled with low fees. The Schwab Premier Income Fund will appeal to conservative retirement-minded investors who might otherwise be lured to annuities. The fund is invested primarily in conservative short-term bonds and stocks, but also includes smaller amounts in more speculative investments which carry greater risk, but can provide greater returns.

Is there any advantage to owning a variable annuity as compared to owning mutual funds?

Yes, there is one. Aggressive investors can move money among their annuity's sub-accounts freely and without incurring any income taxes as they rebalance their investment portfolio of sub-accounts within the variable annuity. Outside of an annuity, cashing in some or all of a mutual fund and switching the proceeds to another mutual fund cannot be done without incurring a tax liability. However, this advantage is not as significant as it might seem. Most people are better served not chasing after the segment of the market that is in favor for the moment, but instead making a well-reasoned asset allocation and then sticking to it, fine tuning it perhaps annually to maintain a precise asset allocation, rather than chasing after today's flavor-of-the-day sector that rarely is the flavor in favor tomorrow. Chasing after yesterday does not get you to tomorrow any faster.

Ultimately, the choice is clear. Mutual funds are a better investment than a variable annuity.

TRUTH 28

Annuities and asset allocation

"Just as a cautious businessman avoids investing all of his capital in one concern, so wisdom would probably admonish us also not to anticipate all our happiness from one quarter alone."

—Sigmund Freud

If investing were a science, scientists would be rich. Unfortunately for scientists, investing is not a science. Some may prefer to call investing an art, others a crap shoot; but regardless of how you characterize it, successful investing for retirement is a critical activity.

Although investing suffers from no lack of impassioned theorists, it frankly is not subject to rational predictions upon which you can rely in making all your investment decisions. It may be because the return on investments all too often are dependent upon the mentality of irrational investors. Whatever the reason, there is no shortage of investment theories. Some even work in the short run, but the truth is that no particular investment strategy is guaranteed to always provide you with the best investment returns at any particular time.

Too often, investors looking for the quick, easy way to riches follow the hot segment of the market at the moment. This is generally a recipe for disaster because by the time such investors get involved in a particular segment of the market, it is already probably too late to get the most gains. They have violated one of the fundamental rules of investing, which is "buy low, sell high." It sounds easy, but it can be hard to achieve.

How do you determine what the hot segment of the market will be?

The answer is, you don't. Sure, you could try such theories as the hemline theory, in which the stock market follows the hemlines of women's skirts. The higher the hemlines, the higher the market will trend. The lower the hemlines, the worse the stock market and the time to invest in other investments. Trying to find logic in this theory, some have posited that hemlines may reflect the relative optimism of society, which certainly could be a factor in the stock market.

A broken clock is right twice a day—and many of these investment theory dogs have had their day—but in the long run, there does not seem to be any system that is foolproof. It may be that there are just too many fools, or perhaps it is that the financial markets are just plain irrational. Whatever the

There is no one investment theory that will always provide the optimum return on your investments.

reason, there is no one investment theory that will always provide the optimum return on your investments.

So, don't curse the darkness. Light a candle, or at least grab a flashlight.

That light is asset allocation. It works. There may be years that it doesn't work as well as hemline investing, but in the long run (which is what you should be interested in), it will provide you with a steady path to riches. Asset allocation involves apportioning your investment dollars among a variety of different investments. Think of it as betting on more than one horse in the Kentucky Derby; it increases your chance of betting on the right horse to cross the finish line first. Your investments will be divided among the usual suspects: stocks, bonds, and cash (often in the form of better-paying money market funds). How much you allocate to each of these segments is dependent on your individual tolerance for risk. How comfortable are you in taking a risk on investing more in stocks that can provide the possibility of greater returns on your investment dollars, but also carry the possibility of losing value and costing you money? Your tolerance for risk is not necessarily related to your age. You may be more aggressive as an older investor or more conservative as a younger investor. Generally, however, the older you are, the less likely you are to invest aggressively, because the danger in making a wrong decision is magnified when you do not have the years to make up for a decision that, in retrospect, was not a good choice. But most people also have to be wary of investing too conservatively. The days of people retiring and merely cutting the coupons off of their bonds are long gone. People living longer in retirement need the growth potential provided by investing in the stock market. Putting money exclusively in conservative Certificates of Deposit and bonds is just a recipe for going broke at a slower rate, as their investments fail to keep pace with inflation.

Asset allocation involves apportioning your investment dollars among a variety of different investments.

When it comes to the stock portion of your asset allocation, there is a myriad of confusing options available, but you would be wise to heed the advice of Henry David Thoreau when he said, “Simplify, simplify, simplify.” He may not have intended to be talking about modern portfolio management, but good advice is good advice. The strategy of using a variety of low cost index mutual funds to form the basis of your stock holdings is a simple strategy that has one major advantage over other competing strategies—it works. Index funds will allow you to invest in stocks both here in the U.S. as well as in emerging markets abroad, such as China and India. They provide you with tremendous diversification. To return to my example of betting on the Kentucky Derby, with index funds, you again have more horses in the race. And as Martha Stewart would say, “That is a good thing.” (Not that you should take investment advice from Martha Stewart, but once again, good advice is good advice.)

Of course, the key thing in investing, particularly for the long run, is that it is not what you make that is important—it is what you keep. Many investments, even most mutual funds, carry such heavy fees that they eat into the value of your investments. Not so with index funds. The fees and costs that you pay are lower than all other comparable investments. Much more of your money is working for you, and as that money compounds over time, your investment looks better and better.

Of course, the key thing in investing, particularly for the long run, is that it is not what you make that is important—it is what you keep.

So where do annuities fit in your asset allocation?

An annuity that provides you with a guaranteed, regular source of income in retirement not only provides you with a sense of security, but also permits you to be more aggressive in the stock portion of your investment portfolio. You are in a position to take greater risk for greater reward because you have a significant portion of your income needs covered by your annuity.

TRUTH 29

Asset allocation and laddering annuities

"He who hesitates is poor."

—Mel Brooks

Asset allocation is an important part of investing. People are living longer now, and the old portfolio of fixed income securities such as CDs or bonds, with which many elderly investors were comfortable, just won't provide the growth necessary for many people to live comfortably. They need the potential for growth that comes with stock ownership. But stock ownership comes with risk. The value of stocks can go down, sometimes tremendously. So, how do you determine just how much of your portfolio should be in stocks and how much should be in more conservative fixed income investments?

A number of rules of thumb are used to determine the optimum division of stocks and fixed income investments. One formula determines the amount of fixed income investments in your portfolio by multiplying your age by 80%, with the remainder of your portfolio to be held in stock or mutual funds. For example, according to this formula, a 65-year-old person should have 52% of his assets in fixed income investments and 48% in individual stocks or mutual funds.

One formula determines the amount of fixed income investments in your portfolio by multiplying your age by 80%, with the remainder of your portfolio to be held in stock or mutual funds.

There is no magic formula that applies to everyone, but this formula gives you at least some guidance in how to allocate your investments so as to best provide both security and the potential for growth.

Climbing to a secure retirement on a laddered investment approach is nothing new. Many conservative investors have used a ladder approach when buying Certificates of Deposit to help provide for a higher rate of return on their investments in a world where you never know which way interest rates are headed. At any one time, the longer you tie up your money in a CD, the higher the interest rate the bank will give you. However, if you buy a long-term CD in a time of lower interest rates, the earning power of your investment is somewhat diminished. Consequently, what some people do to hedge against this possibility is to buy a series of CDs. For example, they buy five CDs, with the first maturing after one year, the second maturing after two years, and so on. As each CD matures, they replace it with a new CD that matures in five years. In this way, they have liquidity and access to their funds in a CD maturing every year, while overall, they get returns close to the rate that they would get for a single five-year CD.

Another way to ladder the fixed income portion of your portfolio is to use fixed income immediate annuities. Whereas a variable annuity is a retirement investment used to grow a tax-deferred nest egg for a later retirement many years down the road, a fixed immediate annuity is one that you purchase at the time of your retirement to provide a steady source of income that is guaranteed for years or even for life. Fixed immediate annuities will not protect you against inflation because their rate of return is indeed fixed; however, for an extra price, you may be able to purchase inflation protection within your fixed immediate annuity. The only problem here is that not only do you pay an additional fee for this extra feature, but also the regular monthly annuity payments from the insurance company to you are reduced.

However, regardless of the fact that there may not be an inflation adjustment for money that you invest in a fixed immediate annuity, there is a tremendous feeling of satisfaction knowing that the fixed immediate annuity that you buy to pay you for life will indeed do so regardless of how long you live. In fact, knowing that you will have this consistent source of income for the rest of your life may put you in a position to feel more comfortable investing the growth portion of your portfolio more aggressively in stocks or mutual funds. With fixed income immediate annuities, there is no such concern about the safety of your investment.

Just as with CDs , you may be concerned about interest rates possibly rising, and that if you lock yourself into a lower paying annuity because you timed your purchase "wrong," you may be losing out on a greater potential return on your investment. With CDs , the way you minimize this risk is through laddering, as I described previously. So, how do you ladder your investments in fixed immediate annuities as you might with CDs ? One way to do that is to divide the money you would otherwise use to buy a fixed immediate annuity and instead buy your annuities over a period of years. For instance, you might buy lifetime annuities over the next four years, with each annuity being bought with 25% of the money you are allocating to the fixed income portion of your portfolio of investments. By utilizing this strategy, you will not only put yourself in a position to take advantage of possibly rising interest rates, but in addition, because the amount you are paid on a fixed income immediate annuity is related to your age, the older you are, the more the insurance company will pay you for your annuity purchase. Consequently, there is an advantage to putting off buying annuities for your income needs in retirement. The later in life you buy the annuity, the more the insurance company is willing to guarantee that they will pay you.

One thing that laddering annuities will do for you and your asset allocation that laddering CDs will not do is guarantee that you will receive payments for the rest of your life. No CD can provide you with that guarantee.

One thing that laddering annuities will do for you and your asset allocation that laddering CDs or bonds will not do is guarantee that you will receive payments for the rest of your life.

If you do decide to ladder your annuity purchases by buying three or four lifetime annuities, you may also consider spreading out your purchases among three or four different annuity issuers because once you get a fixed immediate lifetime annuity, you are entering into a (hopefully) long relationship with that company. Spreading your purchases among a number of different companies helps insure that your retirement will not be totally dependent upon the financial stability of any one company.

TRUTH 30

Minimum required distributions

“The Lord giveth and the IRS taketh away.”

—Anonymous (he didn’t want to get audited)

The federal government, in general, and the IRS, in particular, enact laws and write regulations to encourage people to save for retirement. One of the primary ways that we are encouraged to save for retirement is by making certain investments tax-deferred.

No one likes paying taxes. So, tax laws and regulations encourage us to save for retirement by permitting us to put money into various saving vehicles, such as traditional IRAs, 401(k)s, and annuities that defer taxes. They promise us that in return for being responsible citizens and saving our money for our sunset years, we can put off paying any taxes on all the income that we earn from these various tax-advantaged retirement investment vehicles until some later date. The advantage of such tax deferral is that not only do we avoid paying income taxes while younger, but at the time that we do eventually pay income taxes, we may be in a lower tax bracket. Even when we do pay taxes on investment profits that have had the opportunity to grow faster by not being reduced by income taxes for years, our tax bills may be considerably lower.

But all good things must come to an end and, with the notable exception of investments in Roth IRAs, you are ultimately required to start taking money out of your traditional IRA or 401(k) at age 70 ½, and at that time, pay the income taxes on the money that you take out of these accounts. In keeping with IRS policy, the rules for the minimum amount that you must take out of these tax-deferred accounts is made as ridiculously complicated as possible so that, in fact, you are not actually required to take out the money in the year that you turn 70 ½, but rather you can postpone taking your first minimum required distribution out of your IRA until April Fools Day of the year after the year you turn 70 ½. If that makes sense to you, you must be a Congressperson. But let's not leave it there. Let's complicate things further. That first distribution

You are required to start taking money out of your traditional IRA or 401(k) at age 70 ½, and at that time, pay the income taxes on the money that you take out of these accounts.

that you are required to take for the year that you turn 70 ½ may be taken in the next calendar year, but the distribution for the second year must be taken by December 31st in that year. This means that if you do put off taking your first distribution until the year after you turn 70 ½, you will end up having to take two distributions in one year. This could have a potentially adverse affect on your income tax bill by putting you into a higher tax bracket, not to mention the fact that increasing your income in that fashion could also lead to as much as 85% of your Social Security benefits being subject to income tax.

Calculating how much you need to take from your IRA or 401(k) account is surprisingly easy.

Calculating how much you need to take from your IRA or 401(k) account is surprisingly easy. Of course, for many people, it is easy because we have other people do it for us—either our IRA custodian or our 401(k) plan administrator. However, it is a good idea to know how these calculations are done, both so that you can confirm the accuracy of their figures, as well as to be able to project future withdrawals and plan ahead.

In 2002, the IRS revamped and simplified the method for calculating minimum required distributions. You start your calculations by taking the balance of your IRA account or 401(k) account as of December 31st of the previous year. Then you divide that number by the figure corresponding to your age in the IRS Uniform Lifetime Table. For example, if your traditional IRA contained $100,000 and you were age 71, the divisor figure from the Uniform Lifetime Table is 26.5, which when applied to your IRA account balance would result in a minimum required distribution amount of $3,773.58 for that year. Each year, you repeat the process by applying the divisor figure that corresponds to your age in that particular year. The Uniform Lifetime Table goes all the way up to 115. For those people reaching the age of 116 or older, the IRS gives a Senior Citizen discount and merely applies the divisor figure for someone 115 years of age, which is 1.9.

However, if your spouse is more than ten years younger than you and she is the sole beneficiary of your IRA, you may use the Joint Life Expectancy Table or, as I refer to it, the Derek Table (named after John

Derek, the Hollywood actor and director, who managed to wed, in order, three gorgeous actresses: Ursula Andress, Linda Evans, and Bo Derek, all of whom were at least ten years younger than him at the time of their marriages). For example, if the 71-year-old man from the example in the previous paragraph were married to a 50-year-old woman, he would have a divisor of 35 according to the Derek Table, so his minimum required distribution would be $2,857.14.

Of course, these calculations are only for minimum required withdrawals. There is nothing preventing you from taking out more than your minimum required distribution amount in any year that you choose. The only drawback is that whatever amount you withdraw from your traditional IRA or 401(k) is subject to income tax in the year that you take out the money. And the money that you take out in excess of your minimum required distribution amount in any particular year cannot be applied to reduce the amount that you are required to take in the next year.

However, when it comes to annuities, none of these calculations apply. Although, as with traditional IRAs and 401(k)s, there are restrictions and tax-penalties that apply to withdrawals before the age of 59 ½, there are no requirements that you must take out money from your annuity at any time, although some companies may require you to start taking money out of your annuity at age 85. For the most part, however, if you wish, you can leave your money in your annuity to grow tax-deferred as long as you want.

TRUTH 31

About 59 ½

"I don't make jokes. I just watch Congress and report the facts."

—Will Rogers

When it comes to magic numbers, 59 ½ has it all over magic numbers in professional sports. In professional sports, toward the end of a season, a magic number provides fans with something new to obsess about as they mull over how many games their favorite team would have to win to assure themselves of winning a championship. For example, if the Red Sox are leading the Yankees in the standings in the last week of the season and have a magic number of three, it means that any combination of three Red Sox wins or Yankee losses would make the Red Sox the division champions.

When it comes to annuities, like traditional IRAs and 401(k)s, the magic number is 59 ½. This is the minimum age you must be to withdraw money from your annuity, traditional IRA, or 401(k) account without being assessed a 10% penalty by the IRS in accordance with federal law.

When it comes to annuities, like traditional IRAs and 401(k)s, the magic number is 59 ½. This is the minimum age you must be to withdraw money from your annuity, traditional IRA, or 401(k) account without being assessed a 10% penalty by the IRS.

But why 59 ½? The answer goes back to the earliest of Congress's attempts to encourage private retirement savings, the Keogh Plan. A *Keogh Plan* is a tax-deferred retirement account into which self-employed people are permitted to put large amounts of their net earnings. New York Congressman Eugene Keogh pioneered the concept in 1962. When the idea was being debated in Congress, much of the debate centered on the question of what would be the proper age to permit people to have access without a penalty to the money saved in a Keogh Plan. Congress' intention was to balance the federal government's need for tax revenues with advancing the concept of encouraging private individuals to take the initiative in regard to their own retirement. The early withdrawal penalty was intended to serve as a disincentive for people to use the money for purposes other than their retirement.

In the debate in both the Senate and the House of Representatives, the age of sixty (a nice, round, even number) was mentioned as being the common retirement age at the time. However, it appeared that in insurance company actuary years (as contrasted with dog years), the age of sixty was actually 59 ½. So Congress decided not to reinvent the wheel and used the accumulated experience of the actuaries to determine what the proper minimum age should be to permit non-penalized withdrawals from Keogh Plans. In this way, Congress placed itself in conformity with insurance policies that utilized half-year accounting to determine "insurance age." The life expectancy for men and women back in 1962 was just about 70 years, while the average age of retirement at that time was 60. Now, the life expectancy of the average American is approximately 78 years; for men, the average retirement age is 62, and for women, it is 61. However, perhaps due to not saving enough or maybe just because they are living longer and healthier, 30% of Americans between the ages of 65 and 69 are still working, as compared to only 18% of people between the ages of 65 and 69 who were still working in 1985.

Congress placed itself in conformity with insurance policies that utilized half-year accounting to determine "insurance age."

Of course, stacking the deck when it comes to setting retirement ages is nothing new. In 1935, when Social Security was first enacted, the age of 65 years was set as the age to receive full retirement benefits. At that time, most people may not have been aware that the average life expectancy was a little under 62 years, so the system was geared toward substantial numbers of people not living long enough to make claims.

In any event, the magic number of 59 ½ has managed to stand the test of time and has not only remained unchanged in regard to early withdrawals without a penalty from a Keogh Plan, but was later adopted and maintained to this day for annuities, traditional IRAs and 401(k)s. "Traditional" is an interesting word to describe the legislation for IRAs, which have only been around since 1975. Although in Baby Boomer years, 1975 was not that long ago, to Generation Xers and others, it may seem like an eternity ago.

As for the age of 70 ½—which is the age at which a participant in a traditional IRA or 401(k) must begin to take withdrawals from his or her tax-deferred account—you would think that Congress was just being consistent, and that 70 ½ was the actuarial equivalent of 70, but you would be wrong. Interestingly, 70 ½ is not "insurance age" for 70, although a report of the Social Security Administration done in 1960 indicated that the average life expectancy of men who would be contributing to self-employed retirement plans was 70.45 years. In any event, like 59 ½, the 70 ½ magic number has managed to stand the test of time as well and is still used as the latest age for the commencement of mandatory withdrawals from a Keogh, annuity, traditional IRA, or 401(k) account. However—and I don't mean to confuse you—precisely speaking, the maximum age to which withdrawals may be delayed is not 70 ½. According to the law, distributions from an IRA, Keogh, or 401(k) must commence no later than April Fool's Day in the calendar year following the year in which the owner of such tax-deferred plans reaches the age of 70 ½. However, although the plan owner can defer taking his or her first payment until the year after he or she turns 70 ½, he or she must also take a distribution from his or her IRA, Keogh, or 401(k) for that calendar year as well, which could bring about adverse income tax consequences. As for annuity owners, they do not generally have to concern themselves with this problem because most annuities do not have a maximum age at which withdrawals must be commenced.

Most annuities do not have a maximum age at which withdrawals must be commenced.

TRUTH 32

Annuities in IRAs

"Too much of a good thing can be wonderful."

—Mae West

Mae West may have been right in some circumstances, but her comment certainly does not apply to putting an annuity into an IRA. In fact, it is far from wonderful—it is downright foolish. About the only one who profits from that scenario is the salesperson who sells you the annuity.

Perhaps the most positive aspect of an annuity is that the money grows tax deferred, so you do not pay income taxes during the years that the annuity is in the accumulation phase. This, in turn, permits more of your money to compound and ultimately earn you a greater return than many other investments.

But does it?

As always, remember my mantra, "It is not what you make that is important—it is what you keep." Unfortunately, when it comes to annuities, there are two main drains on what you will get to keep from your investment. First, the fees found in variable annuities dwarf those of similar investments, which in turn, ultimately reduces what you get to keep. In addition, when you do finally start taking money out of your variable annuity, the earnings that you withdraw are taxed at higher ordinary income tax rates rather than the drastically lower capital gains rates that you would pay if you had invested in mutual funds that were pretty much identical to those that made up the sub-accounts of your variable annuity.

However, that tax deferral is still hard to ignore. But it becomes easier to ignore when you consider putting an annuity into your IRA, whether it is a traditional IRA or a Roth IRA, because both of those types of IRAs are already tax-advantaged investments. There is absolutely no tax advantage whatsoever to owning an annuity in an IRA, just as there is absolutely no tax advantage whatsoever to owning tax-free municipal bonds in an IRA. And if you take away the advantages of tax deferral from an annuity, you really have little else to recommend it.

There is absolutely no tax advantage whatsoever to owning an annuity in an IRA.

Another important factor that may be overlooked when having an annuity in a traditional IRA is that the required date for you to start taking distributions—which is the April Fool's Day following the year in which you reach the age of 70 ½—may, depending on when you purchased the annuity, occur during your surrender penalty period. This would cause you to be subject to financial penalties from the insurance company if you take your required distribution.

But let's give the devil his due. What possible other reasons could there be to hold an annuity in an IRA other than to help fund the college expenses of the annuity salesperson's children? Well, you might hear that an annuity has a beneficiary designation, so that if you die, the value of the annuity goes to whomever you choose without being subject to probate. Without even getting into the question of how expensive and time consuming probate is for most people, the truth is that IRAs already are set up with beneficiary designations that will avoid probate. Thus, once again, the so-called advantage of the annuity provides nothing that you would not already have with any IRA investment and, most importantly, at much less cost associated with other investments.

IRAs already are set up with beneficiary designations that will avoid probate.

How about annuitizing the policy, where you start to take regular payments from your annuity so that it can provide you with a secure income stream for life. Surely that is an advantage. Indeed, this may be perceived as a valuable advantage by many people. Of course, that goal may be achieved, and again at less cost, by merely investing in low-cost index mutual funds in your IRA, and then at the time of your retirement, taking the money out of your IRA to purchase an immediate fixed annuity.

Finally, the insurance companies play their last card when it comes to urging you to put an annuity into your IRA by telling you that there is a death benefit (there it is again, that oxymoron) tied to your annuity that no mutual fund can ever offer. The salesperson tells you that your deferred annuity has a life insurance component that will pay your designated beneficiaries the greater of all your contributions to the annuity or the value of the account. With a variable annuity, the value of your account is tied to the mutual funds that make up the sub-accounts within your annuity. So, if the market took a downward turn at the same time that you did (a euphemism for dying), it is possible that the value of your annuity could be less than what you invested into it, particularly when you consider all the fees and costs inherent in having maintained the annuity. With the death benefit, it appears that you are guaranteeing that your heirs will not ever receive less than you invested in the annuity.

But at what cost?

Remember my mantra, "It is not what you make that is important—it is what you keep." There are no free lunches, no free breakfasts, not even a free scone, and you certainly do not get life insurance coverage through your annuity at no cost to you. The truth is that the cost of this insurance is quite expensive to you when compared to insurance coverage that you could obtain on your own outside of the annuity. Of course, the fee that you pay for the insurance premium portion of your annuity just further reduces the value of your investment, as more of it goes to cover the insurance premium and is not there to become a part of your growing investment. This fee in your annuity is called a Mortality and Expenses charge (M & E). It is not unusual for this fee to be as much as 1.75%. So, if you had a $100,000 annuity with a 1.1% M & E charge, you would be charged $1,100 each year just for your insurance coverage. This fee is in addition to the management fees and other fees associated with your annuity, and it certainly puts a crimp in the value of your account. When you think about it, you are not even getting life insurance of $100,000 in our example, unless the stock market does a total crash and the value of your annuity plummets to nothing. What is being insured is just the amount your annuity loses if the sub-accounts in your annuity go down in value. What if, as generally happens over time, the value of the stock market, and correspondingly your annuity's sub-accounts, increase in value? In that case, you continue to pay year after year for insurance for which you have no need whatsoever.

So, maybe Mae West was wrong after all. Or perhaps she was right when she said, "An ounce of performance is worth a pound of promises." Annuities in IRAs make promises they can't keep.

TRUTH 33

Annuities and 401(k)s

"'Tis said that persons living on annuities are longer lived than others."

—Lord Byron

Although investing in an annuity inside an IRA probably does not make sense for anyone other than the person selling you the annuity, investing some of your 401(k) money in an annuity may make sense for some people.

As always, the attraction of an annuity is to have a guaranteed investment for people who are fearful of outliving their savings. Although it is not advisable to put all of your 401(k) eggs in the annuity basket, having a portion of your 401(k) invested in an annuity may let some people sleep a bit better at night.

One of the main benefits to purchasing an annuity through a 401(k) relates to one of the major drawbacks to buying an annuity outside of a 401(k). The fees for buying an annuity through a 401(k) are considerably cheaper than buying an annuity on your own. Additionally, annuities purchased within a 401(k) account do not carry surrender charges, which can be a considerable disincentive to the purchase of an annuity. However, it certainly should be noted that although the fees for buying an annuity through a 401(k) are much less than buying one on your own, the fees involved with an annuity as a 401(k) investment are certainly much higher than the cost of other investments available to you in your 401(k). As always, what you make in a particular investment is not nearly as important to you as what you get to keep. And what you get to keep is dramatically affected by the management fees and other costs associated with a particular investment. When it comes to investing success, annuities will always be a bit behind other investments because of the fees involved.

Annuities purchased within a 401(k) account do not carry surrender charges.

Another benefit of buying an annuity within a 401(k) account rather than on your own outside of your 401(k) is that unlike purchasing an annuity privately, when you buy it through your 401(k), you do so with pretax money. That is, the money you earned and use to purchase the annuity is not subject to income tax in the year that you buy the annuity through your 401(k). With a private purchase of an annuity outside of a 401(k), you are income taxed on the money you earned to pay for the annuity.

Another benefit of buying an annuity within a 401(k) account rather than on your own outside of your 401(k) is that unlike purchasing an annuity privately, when you buy it through your 401(k), you do so with pretax money.

Sellers of annuities often tout the fact that they are a tax-advantaged investment. The interest earned through your annuity grows income tax-deferred until you take the money out of the annuity. They generally do not make a point of telling you that when you do take the money out of your annuity, it is subject to income tax at high ordinary income tax rates rather than the lower capital gains rates that you would pay for a mutual fund investment, but that is a topic for another Truth. Similarly, investments in 401(k) accounts are also tax deferred. You do not pay income taxes on the earnings of your 401(k) until you take the money out. Opponents of the use of annuities in 401(k) accounts often point out the fact that there is no advantage to putting a tax-deferred investment in a tax-deferred retirement plan. However, they may miss the point that a fixed annuity may be worth having in a 401(k) if the costs are right, for the security and stability it brings to your retirement planning—not to mention the value of having an annuity working for you in your 401(k), growing and deferring taxes for many years, and thereby making its return that more valuable to you.

Fixed annuities just might be an appropriate investment for some people in a 401(k) account. As with all fixed annuities, the prevailing interest rates and your age at the time you invest your money help determine the amount that you ultimately receive from your annuity. Starting your investment in an annuity within a 401(k) early in your working career can ultimately help you earn more than if you waited until you retire to invest the money in a fixed annuity. Generally, with a fixed annuity in a 401(k) account, the payments to you from the annuity are based upon conservative investments by the insurance companies issuing the annuity in bonds and other fixed-income securities. Fixed annuities are bought by people concerned with the safety of their investment. They may be people who are entirely conservative in their investment risk tolerance or they may be people who wish to have a guaranteed base for their retirement planning and are willing to take greater risks with the balance of their retirement funds. As with all annuities, you will pay income taxes at ordinary income tax rates when you start to receive payments from the annuity contained in your 401(k).

In contrast to fixed annuities, which are safe investments that are comparable to Certificates of Deposit, variable annuities are speculative investments. The amounts that you receive in return for your investment are dependent upon the performance of the mutual funds that make up the sub-accounts of your annuity. Here, however, the fees that come with a variable annuity make it imprudent to invest in one in your 401(k). You can invest in comparable mutual funds directly through your 401(k) without the myriad of additional fees to which you will be subjected if you purchase a variable annuity in your 401(k), not to mention the adverse income tax problems that occur when you start taking money out of the annuity.

Ultimately, you may determine that you do not want to have your 401(k) money invested in annuities during your working years. However, there is nothing that prevents you from taking the money from your 401(k) at retirement and rolling it over into an IRA, through which you purchase a fixed immediate annuity that will provide you with income for the rest of your life.

TRUTH 34

More about annuities, IRAs, and 401(k)s

"You cannot escape the responsibility of tomorrow by evading it today."

—Abraham Lincoln

Before you invest in an annuity with all its attendant fees and taxes, you should maximize your investments in other tax-advantaged retirement vehicles that may be available to you. Two of the more common and important retirement investments for which you may be eligible are a 401(k) and an IRA.

The most common retirement account provided by employers is the 401(k) account. In a conventional 401(k) account, you are allowed to contribute a portion of your salary, such as 10%, into a tax-deferred retirement account. The money that you contribute from your salary into your 401(k) account is pre-tax. Income taxes are deferred until you take the money out of your account. In addition, many companies will match all or a portion of your annual contribution to your 401(k), thereby giving you, in essence, free money that is added to your 401(k) account to grow tax-deferred.

In 2008, the maximum amount that, by federal law, you could contribute to your 401(k) was set at $15,500. People over the age of 50 are allowed to contribute an additional $5,000, for a total of $20,500 to their 401(k) accounts. These limits, however, are subordinate to any lesser levels set by the particular 401(k) plan at your place of employment. Although an annuity, like a 401(k), will provide tax deferral, you do not get the benefit of matching funds with an annuity. In addition, the purchase of your annuity is done with after-tax dollars, so a 401(k) is definitely a better choice if you are choosing between the two.

In addition to the regular 401(k), your employer may also offer a Roth 401(k) that functions like a Roth IRA. Similar to a Roth IRA, the money you use to fund your Roth 401(k) is after-tax money, so it does not provide you with the initial tax benefit of a regular 401(k). However, like a Roth IRA, when you withdraw the money, it comes out totally tax-free after years of compounding and growing tax-free. Unlike the regular 401(k), employer-matching funds may not be contributed to a Roth 401(k). For those of you who have difficulty making up your mind or prefer to look at it as diversifying your retirement investment strategies, you can have both a regular 401(k) and a Roth 401(k) at work. However, although you may divide your contributions between the two, the total that you contribute to both 401(k)s may not exceed your plan's annual limit.

When it comes to IRAs, your choice is once again between the traditional IRA and a Roth IRA. The law permits you to contribute money to a traditional IRA while generally getting a deduction for your contribution, a benefit that no annuity can offer. In a traditional IRA, your investment grows tax-deferred, and you pay income taxes on your investment when you take money out of your IRA. When you put money into a Roth IRA, you do so with after-tax money so that there is no initial tax benefit to funding a Roth IRA. In this way, it is similar to an annuity. However, whereas annuities grow tax-deferred, your investment in a Roth IRA grows tax-free. Unlike 401(k)s and traditional IRAs, you are not required at any time to withdraw money from your Roth IRA, if you want to have a tax-free investment that grows for yourself or your family.

The amount that the law permits you to contribute to an IRA, whether it is a traditional IRA or a Roth IRA, is the same $5,000 in 2008. If you are over the age of 50, the law will permit you to invest an additional $1,000 to your IRA in 2008. After 2008, the maximum amount that you will be permitted to contribute to an IRA will be increased in $500 increments based upon inflation.

When compared to either a 401(k), a Roth 401(k), or a traditional IRA, an annuity (particularly when you consider the fees involved) will always come up short, so it is an easy decision to invest first in any of these retirement vehicles before turning to an annuity.

But an annuity does have one thing that these other retirement investment accounts do not have: There is no ceiling on the amount that you can invest in an annuity. In addition, in 2008 there are income limits in order to qualify for a Roth IRA. There is no such income restriction on investing in a tax-deferred annuity. In order to have your contribution to a traditional IRA be tax-deductible, there are income limitations. Therefore, you can put more money into an annuity to be held on a tax-deferred basis than you can with these other retirement account options. Another advantage of an annuity when compared to a traditional IRA is that most companies will permit you to purchase a tax-deferred annuity up until age 85, whereas you cannot set up a traditional IRA once you have reached the magic age of 70 ½. There is no age restriction at all for setting up a Roth IRA.

One way of joining the benefits of a fixed immediate annuity's potential to provide you with a...safe income stream for life... would be to cash out your Roth IRA at retirement...and use the money to buy an immediate fixed income annuity with a guaranteed lifetime payout.

One way of joining the benefits of a fixed immediate annuity's potential to provide you with a safe income stream for life with the benefits of a Roth IRA would be to cash out your Roth IRA at retirement—an event that would not be subject to any adverse income tax consequences—and use the money to buy an immediate fixed income annuity with a guaranteed lifetime payout for yourself and even your spouse. The fixed immediate annuity would be purchased with the large lump sum you obtained by cashing in your Roth IRA, which had grown tax-free for hopefully many years. And now that you may be in a position where you want to reduce your risk, you can invest the money in a fixed immediate income annuity. This annuity will pay you a guaranteed interest rate for anywhere from one to ten years, at which time you can either choose another guaranteed interest rate or agree to go with a renewal rate, as determined by the insurance company issuing your annuity. There is no question that a fixed immediate income annuity is not the kind of investment that will provide you with bragging rights at a cocktail party. (Have you ever wondered about the other investments that those people, who have a need to tell you about their "killings" in the stock market, may have had, which may have only been either mere "flesh wounds" or even just "rug burns?") In any event, making a killer of an investment is not why you get a fixed income immediate annuity. You buy one for the security that it brings for a lifetime.

TRUTH 35

Annuities for children

"Children today are tyrants. They contradict their parents, gobble their food and tyrannize their teachers."

—Socrates

Despite Socrates' lament shared by many parents today, we still try our best to plan for our children's future. Although we more often think of annuities as being an investment choice of older people, children may, in limited circumstances, actually be better candidates for investing in annuities.

Compound interest

The magic of compound interest can be explained in any number of cryptic-looking mathematical formulas, but the concept itself is fairly simple. When you compound interest on any investment, the interest that you receive is added to the original principal invested, so that from the time that you are credited with interest, you now get further interest not just on the original invested principal, but also the interest previously credited. In its worst incarnation, the IRS uses compound interest to turn a small amount of tax owed into a choke-a-horse figure. In its better form, compound interest can increase a long-term investment to astronomic proportions. For example, let's look at a classic example of what was considered a bad deal—namely, the Indians selling of Manhattan to early Dutch settlers for 60 Guilders in 1626. If the Indians had put this money into a Dutch bank at the time and let it ride at 6.5% annually compounded interest, they would have today more than 820 billion dollars, which is more than the value of all the real estate in Manhattan. You may not have a few hundred years as an investment horizon, but regardless of your particular time frame, the longer you can invest, most likely the greater will be your returns. If you manage to avoid income taxes during that investment period so that the amount that is compounding for your benefit is not reduced by income taxes, so much the better.

One of the unwritten rules of thumb for annuity investments is that annuities make sense when held by someone for a period of fifteen years or more who may not need the money before reaching the age of 59 ½. A deferred variable annuity that may be deemed a scam when sold to someone in their 80s, who may not be able to access the money without having to pay a substantial surrender fee for ten years, may be an appropriate investment for a youngster.

Instead of giving gifts to a child, who may initially throw out the gifts and play with the boxes until he or she becomes tired of that as well, you might be serving the child better by putting the money used to pay for those gifts into an annuity that can compound tax-deferred over many years and be available 50 or 60 years later to help fund retirement.

So, are annuities a good investment for children? The answer is a resounding maybe.

The Achilles heel of all annuities, that they turn what would be income taxed at lower capital gains rates of 15% to ordinary income taxed as high as 35%, is just as much of a factor in the consideration to purchase an annuity for a child as an adult. Annuity income is only tax-deferred—it is not tax-free. This leads to another possibility for a child, namely setting up a Roth IRA for the child. Just as it makes sense for an adult to max out other tax-advantaged investments before considering an annuity, it makes just as much sense to consider a Roth IRA for a child before considering investing in an annuity. With a Roth IRA, all of the money put into the IRA and all of the money taken out later in life is tax-free, so not only do you get the benefit of compound interest, you get the benefits of totally untaxed compound interest.

Due to the large amount of fees involved with annuities, it also may make considerable sense (as well as dollars) to invest money on their behalf in index mutual funds. Even though these investments will not be tax-free, such as a Roth IRA, they will not be taxed at ordinary income rates when the child takes out the money from the mutual fund, but rather be taxed at lower capital gains rates. With an annuity, earnings withdrawn by the child would be subject to income tax at higher ordinary income rates.

Roth IRA for children

An attractive alternative to an annuity for a child is a Roth IRA. Setting up a Roth IRA for a child will permit the child to take earnings from a paper route, mowing lawns, babysitting, or even money you pay him or her for doing household chores and contribute up to $5,000 a year to the IRA, where the money can grow and compound tax-free throughout the life of the child. If the child had no other earnings during those early years of contributions to a Roth IRA, he or she would not have to pay any income taxes or Social Security taxes on the wages earned. With the benefits of compound tax-free earnings, even if the child only contributed the maximum amount between the ages of seven and eighteen and then just let the money sit and grow, that child would have millions of dollars available at age 65, totally tax-free. I chose the age of seven for my example because the IRS has recognized that children as young as seven can be paid for work performed. But don't get greedy—play by the rules. If you are going to pay a child to do work, make sure that the child actually does work that is worth the amount the child is paid and make sure that the proper W-2s are filed and proper records kept.

However, there is one scenario in which it might make sense to consider an annuity for a young child. Because annuities are considered retirement accounts, they generally are not considered in the calculation of financial aid for college. A child who does not have enough earned income to have his own Roth IRA could still have money invested in an annuity; this could start him on the road to retirement at an early age without having to be concerned about the investment reducing the amount of financial aid for which the child may otherwise be eligible.

Because annuities are considered retirement accounts, they generally are not considered in the calculation of financial aid for college.

TRUTH 36

Bonus credits

"People may or may not say what they mean...but they always say something designed to get what they want."

—David Mamet

When you were in school, it was always helpful to take advantage of the opportunity to receive extra credit. Consequently, it is easy to understand why people being sold variable annuities are initially attracted to a feature called a "bonus credit." Unfortunately, unlike your days in grade school, a bonus credit does not always work to your advantage.

In an effort to make their annuities appear to be more attractive as an investment, some insurance companies will offer you an optional feature called a "bonus credit." Through this feature, the insurance company offers to add a bonus to the value of your annuity contract. Typically, these bonus credit features will range from 1% to 5% of your payment.

So, for example, if you buy a variable annuity with a payment by you of $100,000, an insurance company offering a bonus credit of 4% will add an additional $4,000 to your account. On the surface, this looks like a great deal. You appear to receive free money from the insurance company that is added to your account to grow and grow while you pay nothing for this bonus.

Or do you?

As you might expect, you are not getting (as Dire Straits sang in their 1985 Grammy-winning song) "money for nothing"—and don't think for a minute that you will be getting, as the song also said, "chicks for free." There are no free bonus credits. You pay for this "free" bonus credit in one of two ways.

The first way is through a surrender fee for the variable annuity with the bonus credit, which may be a larger fee than the norm or be in effect for a longer period of time than the surrender fee contained in a variable annuity issued by the same insurance company through a contract that does not contain a bonus credit. However, if you are truly a long-term investor and are not at all bothered by surrender fees or concerned that you may need to access the money in the annuity for at least ten years, you may wish to consider a variable annuity with this provision.

There are no free bonus credits. You pay for this "free" bonus credit in one of two ways.

The other way that the cost of bonus credits is paid for by you is when the cost is reflected in higher mortality and expense fees. Mortality and expense charges, often referred to as M & E charges, are a regular annual fee that you pay to cover the cost of administrative expenses associated with your annuity, as well as the cost of commissions involved in the sale of your annuity and, perhaps most importantly, to cover the cost of the life insurance component of your annuity. These costs are calculated as a fixed percentage of the value of your annuity. The costs of M & E charges can vary significantly from company to company; however, the average is 1.1%. It is important to note that as the value of your annuity increases over time, so does the amount of money that you are paying for the M & E. Correspondingly, in those situations where an increased M & E charge is used to cover the cost of bonus credits, the cost to you of receiving this "free" benefit also increases.

As the value of your annuity increases over time, so does the amount of money that you are paying for the M & E.

An example of how the additional costs of the "free" benefit can reduce the value of your annuity is provided by the Securities and Exchange Commission on their web site (www.sec.gov/investor/pubs/varannty.htm), where it compares two annuities bought for the same initial purchase price of $10,000. The first annuity offers you a bonus credit of 4%, which certainly on the surface looks attractive because it appears to increase the amount of money initially invested on your behalf by an additional $400. However, the annual fees and charges of the annuity amount to 1.75% of the value of the annuity. In the tenth year of the annuity, the value of this annuity would now be worth $22,978, assuming an annual rate of return before expenses of 10%. The second annuity is one that does not provide any bonus credits, so your initial $10,000 investment is the total amount of money that is working for you in your annuity. Again, assuming a 10% annual rate of return before expenses, but this time assuming the fees and charges associated with the annuity without bonus credits is a lower 1.25%, the value of the second annuity in its tenth year would be $23,136. So, even though you received no bonus enhancements of the amount of your principal invested in the annuity, the fact that the fees charged by the insurance company issuing the annuity without the bonus credits are lower than the fees and charges you are subject to in the annuity offering the bonus credits, is more than enough to compensate for the lack of bonus credits. Once again, one of the critical rules of investing is that it is not what you earn from an investment that is important—it is what you get to keep. The fees, charges, and costs of holding any investment should be factored in every time you compare one investment to another.

There are a number of circumstances under which the insurance company may take away the bonus credits made to you, including your making early withdrawals from the annuity or your death when your annuity contains a life insurance benefit.

Anyone considering exchanging an annuity without a bonus credit feature for another annuity that contains such a feature should be very aware of the effect of such an annuity switch on the applicable surrender period of the new annuity. If you exchange an annuity you own where the surrender period has already tolled, for a new annuity that contains a bonus credit provision, you do not get to carry over the completion of the surrender period of the old annuity to the new annuity. If, for whatever reason, you need to cash in the annuity within the new surrender period, which may be as long as ten years, you may find that you have a significant financial penalty of as much as 8% or more of the value of your new annuity when you cash it in to get at the needed money. Once again, the risks that go along with the bonus credit benefit may not be worth the cost.

The bottom line, as always, is read the fine print. Make sure you understand any and all conditions involved with a bonus credit feature—and don't think for a moment that you are getting something for nothing. Everything has a cost. Do a little digging to find out the financial cost to you of this "free" benefit by comparing the cost of an annuity with a bonus credit benefit to a similar annuity without such a benefit in order to fully understand the true costs.

TRUTH

37

The Pension Protection Act, annuities, and long-term care

"And in the end, it's not the years in your life that count. It's the life in your years."

—Abraham Lincoln

Paying for long-term care is a tremendous concern for many older Americans (and some who are not so old). Long-term care insurance would seem to be an attractive response of the insurance industry to this concern, but it has been met with resistance by many people. Some people consider the premiums high for a product where you only "win" if you go into a nursing home, although you can purchase a policy to provide for at-home care as well—but that doesn't seem like much of a consolation prize.

Generally, long-term care insurance is somewhat analogous to term life insurance in that with term life insurance, you only receive a financial benefit from the policy if you die, which is a tremendous price to pay for getting benefits from your policy. Although it is understood that just as with term life insurance, what you are buying is pure insurance coverage (which, in the case of long-term care insurance, provides funds to be used in the event that the need for long-term care arises), many people are put off by the fact that unlike other types of insurance, such as whole life insurance, you do not build up cash value in the policy that would be available to you during your lifetime for uses other than long-term care. In addition, many people who have waited until later in life to try to purchase long-term care insurance are denied coverage for a host of medical reasons. All in all, for many people, long-term care insurance is not an attractive choice.

But that does not make the problem go away.

Consider the Pension Protection Act of 2006 with another twist on how to purchase long-term care insurance. Under the new law, beginning in 2010, insurance companies will be permitted to issue long-term care insurance as a rider to annuities. This was previously not allowed because the tax laws treated payments from long-term care insurance differently than payments from an annuity. Payments from a long-term care insurance policy are income tax-free, whereas payments from

Under the new law, beginning in 2010, insurance companies will be permitted to issue long-term care insurance as a rider to annuities.

annuities are subject to income tax. The obvious benefit of the new rider is that someone who wants to provide for retirement through an annuity will, come 2010, be able to buy an annuity to help meet that goal. However, that same annuity can also, under the new law, contain a long-term care insurance rider. Thus, the annuity is actually a blending of an annuity with insurance coverage for long-term care needs.

The long-term care insurance rider is far from free, however. The premium for this coverage comes from your tax basis in the annuity. Therefore, if you have an annuity that you bought for $75,000 that is now worth $100,000, your tax basis in the annuity is $75,000. If the premium for your long-term care insurance within this hybrid annuity-long-term care insurance policy is $3,000, your cost basis ($75,000) is reduced by the amount of the premium so that your annuity now has a value of only $97,000. The amount of your taxable gain in the annuity remains $25,000 (the difference between the $97,000 value of the annuity and your costs basis, which is now $72,000). So, when you start to take money out of the annuity, you will still owe income taxes on the earnings over and above what you paid for the annuity at your then-ordinary income tax rates. Meanwhile, although you may take a deduction on your present income tax return for the cost of premiums for long-term care insurance—with the amount of the deduction being dependent upon your age—there is no such deduction for the portion of your annuity that goes to pay for the long-term care insurance component of your annuity. Although this hybrid annuity-long-term care insurance policy does provide a new way of providing for the possibility of long-term care needs, it does not save you any significant taxes in the process, which would be the case if you bought a long-term care insurance policy separately.

However, it should be noted that a person who may not qualify for a separate long-term care insurance policy due to medical conditions, would be able to buy an annuity with a long-term care rider. This could be considered to be a significant opportunity for a person whose health would otherwise disqualify him from eligibility for a long-term care insurance policy to be able to purchase coverage.

An important thing to remember is that these hybrid annuity-long-term care policies will not be available until the year 2010. If you do not want to wait until that time to buy an annuity that you can use

> You can buy an annuity now and then exchange your annuity for a new one in 2010 or later that contains a long-term care insurance rider.

for long-term care insurance, you can buy an annuity now and then exchange your annuity for a new one in 2010 or later that contains a long-term care insurance rider. Fortunately, you can do a 1035 tax-free exchange of your old annuity for the new annuity with the long-term care insurance rider, so that there are no adverse income tax aspects to your exchange of an older annuity for a newer one. For more information about this, see Truth 19, "Tax-Free 1035 Exchanges." However, as with any 1035 tax-free exchange of one annuity for a new annuity, you will not only lose whatever benefits were provided under your old annuity, but also you will be required to pay any still-applicable surrender fees, as well as start a new surrender period for the new annuity. For this reason, for some people—particularly older people—the benefits of the new hybrid policies may not be as great as they appear to be.

TRUTH 38

Annuities and Medicaid

"Nothing has more strength than dire necessity."

—Euripides

Medicare, for which everyone involved in the Social Security system and who is at least 65 years old or disabled is eligible, will only pay for nursing home costs in full for a period of 20 days and with a deductible for the next 80 days. This leaves people needing nursing home care in the unenviable position of having to come up with substantial amounts of money to pay for the cost of a nursing home stay.

That is where Medicaid comes in. Unlike Medicare, it is not a program for which all older Americans are universally eligible. Medicaid is a joint federal-state program, which is the only governmental program that provides significant coverage of the expenses of a person's nursing home expenses. Individuals are only allowed to have minimal assets in order to qualify for Medicaid. This amount, not including the value of a home and a car, is limited to $2,000 of what are referred to in the law as "countable assets." Countable assets may include bank accounts, stocks, bonds, and most other investments. When one member of a married couple goes into a nursing home, the other spouse, referred to in the law as the "community spouse," is permitted to keep an extra amount of their joint assets referred to as the "community spouse resource allowance." This amount is indexed for inflation annually. For 2008, the amount is $104,400. However, any excess of the couples' assets over the amount of the institutionalized spouse's allowance of $2,000 and the community spouse's allowance of $104,400 are generally required to be spent on the care of the institutionalized spouse before he or she would be eligible for Medicaid coverage for his nursing home costs. But not necessarily. That is where Medicaid annuities come in.

An annuity that has been properly structured to comply with the Medicaid regulations is a non-countable asset so that the full amount of the annuity is not considered in determining whether or not an institutionalized person is eligible for Medicaid coverage for nursing home costs. In order to comply with Medicaid regulations,

An annuity that has been properly structured to comply with the Medicaid regulations is a non-countable asset.

an annuity must be immediate, irrevocable, and actuarially sound. This means that the annuity, unlike other types of annuities, may not be cashed in at any time, and it cannot be assigned to anyone else. It also must provide for payments that begin immediately to the community spouse over a period of time no longer than his or her projected lifetime. This is what is meant by the term "actuarially sound."

Annuities that comply with these regulations can be used to protect the assets of a married couple, where one of them is entering a nursing home, and they have too many assets to otherwise qualify for Medicaid coverage. In this instance, the couple must shift ownership of assets in excess of the nursing home resident's $2,000 worth of countable assets and the community spouse's $104,400 worth of countable assets to the community spouse, who then purchases an annuity for his or her benefit. In essence, what the husband or wife does is take assets such as bank accounts and mutual funds that are countable assets and convert them into an asset that is non-countable—an annuity.

Annuities that comply with these regulations can be used to protect the assets of a married couple, where one of them is entering a nursing home, and they have too many assets to otherwise qualify for Medicaid coverage.

Under the provisions of the Deficit Reduction Act, any annuity used for Medicaid-qualifying purposes must also provide that at the death of the community spouse receiving the annuity payments, if there is anything left in the annuity, the state must be reimbursed for all of its Medicaid payments made on behalf of the spouse in the nursing home. However, many estate planners get around this provision of the law and manage to preserve assets for the families of Medicaid recipients by making the term of the annuity for the community spouse as short as possible, so that it is unlikely that he or she will die before receiving all of the payments due from the annuity.

For unmarried people attempting to receive Medicaid coverage, annuities might not look particularly promising at first. This is because unlike the situation where a married nursing home resident may transfer his or her interest in assets to a spouse without any penalty, the transfer of assets from a nursing home resident seeking Medicaid coverage to anyone other than a spouse would be considered a disqualifying transfer and would bring about a substantial disqualification period before the nursing home resident would be eligible for Medicaid. However, there is a scenario where, particularly for people with significant monthly income from Social Security and pensions, their families would benefit from the purchase of an annuity by the nursing home resident.

If, for example, a nursing home resident's pension and Social Security income is $4,000 per month, and the cost of the nursing home is $8,000 per month, he or she would be short by $4,000 of what is required to pay for the cost of nursing home care at the private care rate charged by the nursing home. If the resident was eligible for Medicaid, his or her income, except for a $60 personal needs allowance, would still be required to be applied toward the cost of nursing home care. Medicaid would pay the remaining balance. However, the balance that Medicaid would be paying to the nursing home would not be at the nursing home's private care rate, but rather at the state's reimbursement rate, which is generally significantly less than the private care rate. If, for example, the nursing home resident were to pay $100,000 to purchase an annuity for himself or herself with an actuarially sound five-year payout period, and the nursing home resident died in the nursing home after two years (which is about the average time that a person spends in a nursing home), the state would be required to be reimbursed $49,440 from the remaining balance in the annuity. If, however, the resident had paid for the nursing home costs through the resident's own funds for those two years, $96,000 of his or her assets over and above his monthly income would have had to be used. Therefore, by purchasing the annuity and becoming immediately eligible for Medicaid, the resident would be able to pass on to his or her family at death a considerable amount of money through the remaining three years of the annuity.

TRUTH 39

Annuities and reverse mortgages

"Money, if it does not bring you happiness, will at least help you be miserable in comfort."

—Helen Gurley Brown

Reverse mortgages have become increasingly popular in recent years as a way for house-rich, cash-poor owners of homes, which have dramatically increased in value since they were first purchased, to get access to the equity in their homes to help support themselves.

Essentially, a reverse mortgage, like a conventional mortgage, is a loan that uses your home as security for the loan. However, unlike a conventional mortgage loan—where you borrow money from a bank or other financial institution and then proceed to pay back the loan with interest over a number of years—with a reverse mortgage, you often do not have to pay back the loan with interest until you no longer live in the home. This puts you in a position to tap into your home's value and convert it into cash that you can use to meet your ordinary costs of living without having to be concerned about repaying the loan. Reverse mortgages are generally repaid with interest when the borrower sells the home, moves out of the home, or dies—whichever event occurs first. However, there are some reverse mortgages that are obtained for a specific number of years, after which they must be paid back in full with interest. The amount of money that you can borrow through a reverse mortgage is dependent upon four primary factors: your age, the amount of equity in your home, the applicable interest rate, and the fees rolled over into the loan.

On the one hand, when you borrow money through a reverse mortgage, you do not have to make regular payments of either principal or interest on your loan. When you or your estate does pay back the loan, however, it is with interest that has been compounding for years. As I described earlier in this book, when compound interest works in your favor, as in a deferred annuity, it is a wonderful thing. However, when compound interest works against you, as it does with a reverse mortgage, the final figure of what you eventually owe when your reverse mortgage comes due can be astounding.

The final figure of what you eventually owe when your reverse mortgage comes due can be astounding.

Fees

As always, it is not what you make, it is what you keep that is important.

A reverse mortgage is no exception to this rule. One of the primary objections to reverse mortgages involves what many people see as their excessive fees. It is not unusual for the fees associated with a reverse mortgage to reach between $6,000 and $12,000, which make a reverse mortgage a very expensive way to borrow money. There is a large and wide variety of fees commonly involved in obtaining a reverse mortgage. They include appraisal fees, origination fees, mortgage insurance, credit report fees, flood certification fees, title examination fees, document preparation fees, recording fees, and title insurance fees. They can mount up much faster than the costs of a conventional mortgage. The good news about these fees is that you may be able to avoid paying these fees at the time that you take out the loan by rolling them into the money you are borrowing. The bad news, however, is that not only does rolling over these costs into your loan reduce the amount of money that you are eligible to borrow, but the cost of these fees begin accumulating compound interest from the start of the loan.

Helpful web sites

In order to get a good estimate of what fees might apply to a reverse mortgage you are considering, you can go to the web site of the National Reverse Mortgage Lender's Association at www.reversemortgage.org. For a helpful interactive calculator that can assist you in evaluating a reverse mortgage, you can go to AARP's reverse mortgage web site at www.rmaarp.com.

Reverse mortgage options

If you find yourself in need of extra income to meet the expenses of your everyday life and you do not have other assets to tap into, a reverse mortgage may be a good choice. In order to qualify for a reverse mortgage, all you have to do is be at least 62 years of age and own a home. You do not need to meet any qualifications either as to income or assets in order to qualify for a reverse mortgage, although you can only have one reverse mortgage at a time, and it can only be on your primary residence.

There are a number of private lenders that provide reverse mortgages, although the most popular reverse mortgage is the Home Equity Conversion Mortgage (HECM), sponsored by the Federal

Housing Administration (FHA). There is a tremendous amount of variation of the terms of reverse mortgages; however, your choice of how you take your money breaks down into one of five methods:

1. Monthly payments for a fixed term of years of the mortgage.
2. A tenure plan by which you receive a specific monthly payment for life so long as you occupy the home.
3. An option to utilize the reverse mortgage as a line of credit through which you may have access whenever you need money.
4. A lifetime payment option combined with a line of credit so long as you occupy the home.
5. A lump sum payment.

It should be noted that except for reverse mortgages that are taken out for a specific period of time, the reverse mortgage must be repaid with compound interest at such time as you sell your home, move to a new residence, or die, whichever event happens first—and therein lies the problem. If you outlive the lump sum or credit line funds available to you from the reverse mortgage, or if you have to move or sell your home, you are stuck paying back an enormous debt, while your need for income has probably not diminished.

And that is where combining a reverse mortgage with an annuity comes in. This simple and effective strategy involves taking the money that you obtain through a lump sum reverse mortgage and purchasing an immediate annuity with it. The immediate annuity will pay you income for the rest of your life, regardless of whether you move out of your home or not. The money that you receive from the immediate annuity will be more than the monthly lifetime payments you would get from the reverse mortgage alone, without the condition of having the payments stop if you had to sell your house or move to a new residence.

This simple and effective strategy involves taking the money that you obtain through a lump sum reverse mortgage and purchasing an immediate annuity with it.

TRUTH 40

State Guaranty laws

"If you want a guarantee, buy a toaster."

—Clint Eastwood

People who need people may be the luckiest people in the world, according to Barbra Streisand in *Funny Girl*. People who need guarantees as to the safety of their investments, however, often feel most comfortable when they invest in Treasury Bills and Notes (which are guaranteed by the federal government) or CDs (which are covered by the Federal Deposit Insurance Corporation (FDIC)). In the case of FDIC insurance, if the bank issuing your CD goes bankrupt, you are insured for up to $100,000. In the case of Treasury Bills and Notes, the only way you would not be paid back in full is if the federal government were to fall, in which case we all would have bigger problems than the guarantee of the security of our investments.

But what about annuities?

They are backed by the insurance companies that issue them. As I indicated elsewhere in this book, it is easy to get up-to-date information from a number of different rating services to evaluate the strength and financial stability of any company from which you are considering buying an annuity. But there also are funds maintained by each state government that protect a specific amount of the value of your annuity investment in the unlikely event that the insurance company that issued your annuity becomes insolvent. These State Guaranty funds are funded by mandatory contributions from all the insurance companies doing business within your state. In addition, it should be noted that if your annuity is a variable annuity, the sub-accounts that make up your annuity are required to be kept separate from the insurance company's other assets, and therefore should theoretically not be

But there also are funds maintained by each state government that protect a specific amount of the value of your annuity investment in the unlikely event that the insurance company that issued your annuity becomes insolvent.

in jeopardy if the insurance company that issued your annuity were to become insolvent.

What follows is a list of the various State Guaranty funds and their present limits on the protection of annuities. As with all laws, these may change, which is why I also provide you with the web sites of each of the Guaranty funds to which you can go for current information.

- Alabama: $100,000 (www.allifega.org)
- Alaska: $100,000 (www.aklifega.org)
- Arizona: $100,000 (www.state.az.us/id/)
- Arkansas: $300,000 (www.arlifega.org)
- California: 80% of the value of the annuity not to exceed $100,000 (www.califega.org)
- Colorado: $100,000 (www.lhipa.org)
- Connecticut: $500,000 (www.ctlifega.org)
- Delaware: $100,000 (www.delifega.org)
- Florida: $100,000 (www.flahiga.org)
- Georgia: $100,000 (www.gaiga.org)
- Hawaii: $100,000 (www.hilifega.org)
- Idaho: $300,000 (www.idlifega.org)
- Illinois: $100,000 (www.ilhiga.org)
- Indiana: $100,000 (www.inlifega.org)
- Iowa: $100,000 (www.ialifega.org)
- Kansas: $100,000 (www.kslifega.org)
- Kentucky: $100,000 (www.klhiga.org)
- Louisiana: $100,000 (www.lalifega.org)
- Maine: $100,000 (www.melifega.org)
- Maryland: $100,000 (www.mdlifega.org)
- Massachusetts: $100,000 (www.malifega.org)
- Michigan: $100,000 (www.milifega.org)
- Minnesota: $100,000 (www.mnlifega.org)
- Mississippi: $100,000 (www.mslifega.org)
- Missouri: $100,000 (www.mo-iga.org)
- Montana: $100,000 (www.mtlifega.org)
- Nebraska: $100,000 (www.nelifega.org)
- Nevada: $100,000 (www.nvlifega.org)

- New Hampshire: $100,000 (www.nhlifega.org)
- New Jersey: $100,000 (www.njlifega.org)
- New Mexico: $100,000 (www.nmlifega.org)
- New York: $500,000 (www.nylifega.org)
- North Carolina: $300,000 (www.nclifega.org)
- North Dakota: $100,000 (www.ndliega.org)
- Ohio: $100,000 (www.olhiga.org)
- Oklahoma: $300,000 (www.oklifega.org)
- Oregon: $100,000 (www.orlifega.org)
- Pennsylvania: $300,000 (www.palifega.org)
- Rhode Island: $100,000 (www.rilifega.org)
- South Carolina: $300,000 (www.sclifega.org)
- South Dakota: $100,000 (www.sdlifega.org)
- Tennessee: $100,000 (www.tnlifega.org)
- Texas: $100,000 (www.txlifega.org)
- Utah: $200,000 (www.utlifega.org)
- Vermont: $100,000 (www.vtlifega.org)
- Virginia: $100,000 (www.valifega.org)
- Washington: $500,000 (www.walifega.org)
- West Virginia: $100,000 (www.wvlifega.org)
- Wisconsin: $300,000 (www.wilifega.org)
- Wyoming: $100,000 (www.wlhiga.org)

TRUTH 41

Annuities and creditor protection

"Creditor. One of a tribe of savages dwelling beyond the Financial Straits and dreaded for their desolating incursions."

—Ambrose Bierce

Everyone seems to be worried about being sued, although the litigation explosion that we so often read about is more hype than reality. Many of the lawsuits about which people read are newsworthy just because they are rare, unusual occurrences. In any event, whether the fear is real or not, many people are concerned about protecting their assets from creditors or lawsuits. All the states have laws to protect some or all of the value of a person's home from the claims of creditors through the use of Homestead laws, while other state laws protect life insurance and IRAs (although the laws do differ from state to state).

So, where do annuities stand when it comes to protection from creditors?

The answer is that it depends on the state in which you live. There are considerable differences in the level of protection from state to state. Some states offer no protection whatsoever, while other states offer total protection. The following list describes the protection offered in those states that do protect at least some of the value of an annuity. However, the laws are always changing. If creditor protection is important to you, you should check the laws in effect in your particular home state before you buy an annuity. The law protects:

There are considerable differences in the level of protection from state to state. Some states offer no protection whatsoever, while other states offer total protection.

- Alabama—A maximum of $250 per month of benefits.
- Alaska—A maximum of $12,000 of value of an unmatured annuity.
- Arizona—Only those annuities qualified under Internal Revenue Code sections 401(a), 403(b), 408, and 409.
- California—The whole value of an unmatured policy.
- Connecticut—Only annuities that are ERISA qualified.
- Delaware—A maximum of $350 per month of benefits.
- Florida—The whole value of annuities.

- Georgia—The proceeds of an annuity to the extent that it is reasonably necessary to support the annuity owner and his dependents.
- Hawaii—Amounts payable to the spouse, child, parent, or other dependent of the annuity owner.
- Idaho—A maximum of $1,250 per month of benefits.
- Illinois—Amounts payable to a spouse, child, parent, or other dependent of the annuity owner.
- Indiana—The entire value of the annuity other than payments that resulted from excessive contributions from the prior year.
- Kansas—Annuities the whole value of annuities that qualify under specific state statutes.
- Kentucky—A maximum of $350 per month of benefits.
- Louisiana—The entire value of the annuity; however, the maximum that will be protected is limited to $35,000 if a bankruptcy is filed by the annuity owner within nine months of buying the annuity.
- Maine—A maximum of $450 per month of benefits.
- Maryland—The whole value of the annuity if it is payable to the spouse, child, or dependent relative of the annuity owner.
- Michigan—The whole value of the annuity.
- Minnesota—The whole value of the annuity from the creditors of the annuity owner.
- Mississippi—The value of the annuity to the extent that it is reasonably necessary for the support of the annuity owner and his dependents due to illness, disability, death, or advanced age and the annuity qualifies under Internal Revenue Code sections 401(a), 403(a), 403(b), 408, or 409.
- Missouri—The value of the annuity to the extent reasonably necessary for the support of the annuity owner and his dependents due to advanced age, illness, disability, or death.
- Nebraska—A maximum of $10,000 of the value of the annuity.
- Nevada—A maximum of $350 per month of benefits.
- New Jersey—A maximum of $500 per month of benefits.
- New Mexico—The entire value of the annuity.
- New York—Gives judges discretion to order an amount to be paid to creditors of the annuity owner after considering the reasonable needs of the annuity owner and his dependent family members. The law also provides for a maximum $5,000 exemption if the annuity is purchased within the prior six months.

- North Carolina—Only protects those annuities that qualify under Internal Revenue Code section 408.
- North Dakota—A maximum $100,000 of protection for each individual annuity policy with a total protection amount not to exceed $200,000. However, more may be protected if it is determined that it is reasonably necessary for the support of the annuity owner and his dependents, provided that it is payable to his spouse, children, or other dependent relatives.
- Ohio—The entire value of the annuity where the beneficiary is the spouse, child, or dependent of the annuity owner.
- Oregon—A maximum of $500 per month of benefits.
- Pennsylvania—Annuity payments to the spouse, child, or dependent relative of the annuity owner. The law also protects monthly annuity payments of up to $100 for the annuity owner.
- Rhode Island—Only annuities that qualify under Internal Revenue Code section 408(b).
- South Carolina—Annuities that qualify under Internal Revenue Code section 401(a), 403(a), 403(b), 408, or 409 that are used for payments due to death, disability, or advanced age.
- South Dakota—A maximum of $250 per month of benefits.
- Tennessee—Annuities used to provide for the annuity owner's spouse, child, or dependent relative.
- Texas—The entire value of the annuity.
- Utah—Such amounts of annuities necessary for the reasonable needs and support of the annuity owner and his dependents.
- Vermont—A maximum of $350 per month of benefits.
- Washington—A maximum of $250 per month of benefits.
- Wisconsin—The entire value of the annuity where the annuity payments are made due to advanced age, illness, disability, or death.
- Wyoming—A maximum of $350 per month of benefits.

TRUTH 42

Getting out of an annuity

"If the world was perfect, it wouldn't be."

—Yogi Berra

There can be any number of reasons for getting out of an annuity. You may need the money due to a financial emergency or an adverse change in your health that increases your medical expenses. Or maybe you just realize a particular annuity may not be suited for you. Whatever the reason, annuities are not the easiest things from which to exit easily and gracefully. So let's look at what you are facing and what you can do about it.

Your first problem may be that you are too young. Now I know that for most adults, being too young doesn't seem like that great a problem, but if you are under the age of 59 ½ (and only a Congressperson or a 6 ½-year-old child would think that half years are particularly significant), you run the risk of being assessed a 10% early distribution penalty for prematurely withdrawing earnings from an annuity. Fortunately, there are two ways to avoid this severe financial penalty for early withdrawal. The first way to avoid the penalty is not a particularly attractive one: dying. Yes, it does seem a bit of an extreme tactic merely to avoid paying a 10% tax penalty, but it is true that if you die before the age of 59 ½, you do not have to pay the 10% penalty. Only somewhat of a better alternative is the second way to avoid the penalty, which is by becoming disabled. This may be an important exception, however, because becoming disabled may have a substantial impact on your need for the money sheltered in your annuity.

Or perhaps you want to rid yourself of a particular annuity, not because you are disinclined toward annuities in general, but rather because you may not like the terms or the fees connected with the annuity that you have now. In that case, you can do what is called a 1035 exchange, so named after the applicable section of the Internal Revenue Code. With a 1035 exchange, you are able to cash out one annuity in order to purchase another annuity without a tax penalty. This can be done even if you take the money from one annuity and buy another annuity

With a 1035 exchange, you are able to cash out one annuity in order to purchase another annuity without a tax penalty.

with a different company, perhaps one such as Fidelity or Vanguard, which offers lower-fee annuities. (See Truth 19, "Tax-Free 1035 Exchange," for more details on this option.)

If you are considering an early retirement before the age of 59 ½ and are the owner of a deferred variable annuity, another option available to you would be to exchange your deferred variable annuity for a fixed immediate annuity that would provide guaranteed income for life. Certainly there are fees and expenses connected with fixed immediate annuities, but they are not as great as those connected with deferred variable annuities. The average annual fee for a fixed immediate annuity issued by some of the low-cost annuity companies is only .79%, as compared to an average of 2.39% for the industry average. That is a considerable difference. Think about how much harder your money has to work for you to generate a good profit if fees are taking away 2.39% of the earnings of your annuity every year before you get any benefit.

But even in those situations in which Uncle Sam is not after you for his pound of flesh, the company that issued your annuity is not going to be too thrilled about you leaving. This is particularly true if it is during the surrender period, which can bring about a penalty of seven percent or more and go on for as long as seven years or longer. Once again, your annuity may have a provision for waiver of the surrender fees if you become disabled or go into a nursing home. In any event, annuities generally permit you to withdraw without a penalty a certain amount each year—generally 10% to 15%—even during the surrender charge period, without a penalty.

Maybe you are not totally dissatisfied with your deferred variable annuity but rather are just unhappy with the return you are earning on your investment. In this case, you can just change the mix of investments that you have in the various sub-accounts that make up the investment portfolio of your variable annuity. You can shift assets from one sub-account to another more profitable sub-account without incurring any tax liability due to making the change.

Your annuity may have a provision for waiver of the surrender fees if you become disabled or go into a nursing home.

This can be a significant benefit that you would not have if you shifted investments from one mutual fund to another mutual fund outside of an annuity.

If you believe that you were improperly sold an annuity or that the terms of the annuity were misrepresented to you, you have a number of options. First, you can contact someone in a managerial position in the company that sold you the annuity and demand to cancel the sale of the annuity. If you are unsuccessful in this endeavor, you can contact your state's attorney general to file a complaint, or you can file a complaint with the Securities Industry Regulatory Authority, formerly known as the National Association of Securities Dealers or the Securities and Exchange Commission. You may be in for a long ride, but it may well be worth your while. There have been a number of class actions brought by state officials and regulators on behalf of people to whom annuities were sold improperly that resulted in compensation for the victims of these unfair practices.

Finally, you could just bite the bullet and recognize that the annuity you bought may be an unsuitable investment for you and just get out of it, even if it means taking the tax hit if you are under the age of 59 ½ or still in the surrender charge period. Yes, you will pay for doing this, but is it better to stay in an investment that either was never suitable for you or has become unsuitable for you? You may be better off getting out as soon as you can, taking your losses and getting on with your financial life. Then you can invest in something more appropriate for you so that your money can get back to working for you as best it can.

TRUTH 43

Annuity scams and senior citizens

"I play my part and you play your game.
You give love a bad name."

—Bon Jovi

The sellers of deferred annuities to senior citizens who may not be suitable for deferred annuities don't give love a bad name, but they certainly give a bad name to all the honest annuity salespeople who believe in their products and sell them only to people for whom they may be suited.

The problem with selling deferred annuities to senior citizens is that time may not be on their side—deferred annuities work best only if you indeed do have time on your side.

The trouble with deferred annuities

Immediate annuities, where the person buying it begins receiving payments right away, may be a good and appropriate investment for many seniors. However, a deferred annuity, where you do not begin to receive payments until some time in the future, presents the greatest risk of problems for senior citizens. Taking out more than 10 percent of the money you put into a deferred annuity during a period of as long as 10 years from the time that you first purchased the annuity can often result in significant surrender charges. These charges can pretty much eliminate the benefit of an annuity as an investment for a senior citizen who may have a current or imminent need of the money invested in an annuity (see Truth 5, "Annuity Fees").

The problem with selling deferred annuities to senior citizens is that time may not be on their side, while deferred annuities work best only if you indeed do have time on your side.

The case of Murray Cheves

Old is a relative term. I once had a judge inform me that after many years of changing his standard for what constituted "old," he finally settled in on the standard of "Old is five years older than whatever I am." However, there are very few people who would not have considered Murray Cheves old. Murray Cheves was 90 when a salesman for American Investors Life Insurance Co., a subsidiary of AmerUs Group Co., sold him a $100,000 deferred annuity. Unfortunately for Mr. Cheves, the annuity had surrender charges that dragged on for ten years from the date of issue of the annuity. In order to be able to access his money without a penalty, Murray Cheves would have had to live to the ripe old age of 100. Unfortunately, Mr. Cheves died at age 91, at which time his family had to pay an $11,000 surrender charge to get at the annuity funds. This outrageous situation became the heart of a national class action lawsuit that was eventually settled by AmerUs Group Co.

Unfortunately, the sales tactic of selling annuities with considerable surrender fees to trusting, unsuspecting senior citizens is a problem that exists throughout the country. This has been the basis for many lawsuits brought not just by individual people and groups of similarly situated senior citizens as class actions, but also by a number of state Attorneys General and other state officials.

The crux of the problem is that annuities are a financial product that provides a large commission to the salesperson. Senior citizens often have significant money, which they have accumulated over a lifetime, but are concerned that it may not last for their lifetime. They therefore present a good target for unscrupulous salespeople who see easy sales, regardless of the fact that these perfectly legal investments may not be appropriate to sell to older people due to the surrender charges and other reasons that make deferred annuities inappropriate for many seniors.

Although the surrender charges are probably the most egregious example of a provision that makes deferred annuities inappropriate for many senior citizens, the whole panoply of fees involved with annuities also play a part in turning a legitimate investment into a scam. Scam artist salespeople who sell annuities to older people for whom they may not be appropriate may seek to take all or most of the senior's money and invest it in annuities, rather than consider the annuity to be just one component of a well thought-out financial plan. Even when they are an appropriate investment, annuities should be a component of a well-balanced financial plan utilizing prudent principles of asset allocation and not the sole form of investment.

Many senior citizens first learn about annuities at free seminars, where they become the victims of deceptive and illegal sales tactics. Some seniors are drawn by the "free lunch." Advertising that may prey upon the fear of many seniors that they may outlive their money draws others. Sometimes they are pressured into making quick decisions, which is always something that should make a potential investor wary. Investment decisions should only be made after careful consideration and evaluation of the particular investment. People should never invest in anything that they do not fully understand. Unfortunately, unscrupulous annuity salespeople often press unsuspecting seniors to turn over their money to the salespeople in return for deceptive promises.

Annuities are not necessarily a bad investment choice for seniors. However, immediate annuities are generally the more appropriate annuity product for older people rather than deferred annuities—particularly deferred variable annuities that are inappropriately pushed upon senior citizens for whom these investments are inappropriate.

Having an investment advisor whom you trust or a family member that can help you evaluate investments is a good idea. Older people in particular should recognize their vulnerability and be particularly wary of promises from people they do not know. Trust must be earned. Just because someone gives you a free lunch does not make him or her trustworthy or believable.

Seniors care package

The Securities and Exchange Commission (SEC) has what it refers to as a "Seniors Care Package" of online information or pamphlets that can help you better understand savings, investments, mutual funds, and variable annuities. These are must-have reading for any older American considering purchasing an annuity. They can be obtained at the SEC's web site at http:// www.sec.gov/investor/seniors/seniorscarepackage.htm.

TRUTH 44

Annuities and class actions

"Litigation is the basic legal right which guarantees every corporation its decade in court."

—David Porter

Being classy is a good thing. Being a part of a class action is both a good thing and a bad thing. On the one hand, it means that you share a grievance with many other people similarly situated. You are not alone. Misery may love company. When it comes to a class action, however, it also means that you are part of a lawsuit that combines the clout of many people joined with a generally strong legal team fighting for your rights without your having to contribute much, if anything, toward the case against the company that may have harmed you.

Class actions are lawsuits filed by people who allege that they have been similarly harmed by the particular tactics of a company. Once the court has approved the class as one that is representative of the group of people similarly situated, notices are given to people who might be part of this larger group of people, informing them that they have the opportunity to join the class or to opt out of the class action. By staying a member of the class, individuals are able to reap the benefits of the lawsuit without having to either contribute monetarily toward the lawsuit or to participate actively in the lawsuit. On the other hand, if you stay as a member of the class, you lose your individual right to sue the company that you believe has harmed you. You are bound by the terms of any court judgment or settlement of the class action. In many class actions, victims have found that their compensation received as a member of the class is small. However, this is not a general rule, and every case is specific to its own particular facts.

Variable annuities and equity index annuities have been a source of numerous class actions—not because variable annuities and equity index annuities are in and of themselves illegal or improper, but mostly in relation to the improper marketing of the annuities. This is particularly true as they relate to older people, as well as misrepresentations as to the terms of particular variable annuities and equity index annuities in the course of the sales process.

Variable annuities and equity index annuities have been a source of numerous class actions...in relation to the improper marketing of the annuities.

Some of the common problems that have arisen in the sale of variable annuities and equity index annuities that have been the basis for class actions include the following:

1. Failure of salespeople to properly gather financial information on prospective buyers to determine if such investments are suitable for the prospective buyer.
2. Failure of salespeople to provide information to prospective buyers who are encouraged to do 1035 exchanges of already owned annuities for new annuities being sold by a particular salesperson, who may be making a large commission from a sale where it is inappropriate for the prospective buyer to be exchanging the annuity he already has.
3. Failure of salespeople to inform prospective buyers of important facts about the annuities being proposed by them for sale; specifically, the failure of some companies to properly disclose all of the fees involved, particularly potentially devastating surrender fees and potential IRS penalties for early withdrawals.
4. Misrepresentations of important facts and aspects of the annuities by the salespeople; some examples of misleading advertising involves companies that failed to disclose that variable annuities bought in IRAs or other tax-deferred plans provide no additional tax benefits to the purchaser, and advertising that implied that only annuities would provide tax deferral in already tax-deferred plans such as IRAs.

Perhaps the most egregious misrepresentation that has cropped up in numerous class actions involves the sale of variable annuities and equity index annuities without properly disclosing the surrender periods and charges involved in the particular annuity. In one particular case, a 73-year-old man was convinced to cash in an annuity he already had in order to buy a new annuity that not only started a new surrender period with considerable surrender fees that did not end for thirteen years, but also was not scheduled to begin payments until the man was 115 years old.

A bank robber [Willie Sutton] was once asked why he robbed banks, to which he responded, "Because that is where the money is."

Perhaps the most egregious misrepresentation that has cropped up in numerous class actions involves the sale of variable annuities and equity index annuities without properly disclosing the surrender periods and charges involved.

For many unscrupulous salespeople, selling variable annuities or equity index annuities to unwary seniors makes sense because it makes dollars for them. The temptation to sell these perfectly legal products in illegal ways can be great because the commissions are substantial. It is for this reason that this is a problem which most likely will be with us for a long time. If you do become a victim of improper sales tactics involving a variable annuity or an equity index annuity, you should contact a lawyer. You might consider looking into whether there are other people who have been similarly victimized and who have already started a class action against the company. There are many web sites that can help obtain information; of course, you can always Google the name of the offending company with the words "class action," and you should be able to get the information that you need. Many web sites regarding class actions, however, are maintained by lawyers seeking your business. This is not necessarily a bad thing, but it certainly indicates a bias in the information provided. However, for totally unbiased information on class actions that may affect you, you can go to the Securities Class Action Clearing House web site of Stanford Law School at www.securities.standford.edu.

TRUTH 45

Prospectuses and annuities

"A man who does not think for himself does not think at all."

—Oscar Wilde

Many people first learn about annuities through the compelling advertising that the companies offering these products provide through the various media. Advertising for any financial product always simplifies the product and, of course, makes it look like the best thing since sliced bread (although as George Carlin has noted, "What is so great about sliced bread?").

This is not necessarily a bad thing. Investing is complicated, but like most complicated subjects, it is better to begin your understanding with general knowledge of the concept and then move on to the details. Advertising supplies people with their initial information about investments, but it rarely supplies details. It is important to remember, however, that the devil is in the details. In the case of a prospectus, it is a document that provides all the details, both good and bad, about a financial product. The purpose of a prospectus is to disclose all the terms and conditions of an offer of securities, such as mutual funds or variable annuities, and explain the product so it is understandable. Although the word "prospectus" is not derived from the Greek word for "impossible to understand," a prospectus often has the opposite effect of making the whole process of evaluating a variable annuity even more complicated, if that's possible.

Ultimately, advertising may be understandable, but it is sometimes misleading. A prospectus is far from understandable to people who are not entirely familiar with the complex financial terms and conditions that the prospectus is supposed to disclose and explain.

So, what will you find in a prospectus? It is supposed to provide you with information regarding all the provisions of the annuity—including, but not limited to, the terms and conditions, risks, charges, and expenses involved with the particular annuity. All prospectuses must be filed with the Securities and Exchange Commission. Just because it is filed with the Securities and Exchange Commission does not mean that the SEC has given its stamp of approval to the particular annuity. Not all fixed annuities

A prospectus is far from understandable to people who are not entirely familiar with the complex financial terms and conditions.

are considered securities, but all variable annuities are considered securities and therefore must have a prospectus.

A prospectus for a variable annuity will tell you, among other things:

1. The choice of investment options available to you in the annuity.
2. Definitions of the terms used in the annuity.
3. The fees and expenses.
4. Information about the issuing company.
5. Information about the fixed account and your options as to the fixed account.
6. Information about the accumulation phase and your options as to the accumulation phase.
7. Information about the variable account.
8. Renewal options.
9. Early withdrawal rules.
10. Information about payment options.
11. Account fees.
12. Administrative fees.
13. Distribution fees.
14. Mortality and Expense risk fees.
15. Surrender fees and provisions.
16. Charges for optional riders.
17. Tax information.
18. Death benefits.
19. Optional death benefit riders.
20. Change of ownership provisions.
21. Investment performance information.

In addition to all of this information, there will be a slew of charts and graphs in the prospectus that are supposed to further explain the details of the annuity. The problem is that the prospectus, which is intended to provide a detailed explanation of the annuity you are considering buying, should probably require another prospectus to explain what it means.

As with so many federally mandated disclosure forms, which everyone knows are not often actually read, you will find important information highlighted in dark print to catch your attention. Perhaps most important of this highlighted information is the disclosure that even though the prospectus tells you about the fees and charges involved with the particular variable annuity, this disclosure is not intended to be a representation that these are the actual fees that you will pay both now or in the future. Essentially, what they are telling you is that it is impossible to fully comprehend what the cost will be to you of owning the particular annuity. So, your reward for being one of the few people to actually read the prospectus and come back alive is that you are left perhaps even more confused than when you started.

As Clint Eastwood said in the Dirty Harry movie *Magnum Force*, “A man’s gotta know his limitations.” Unless you are a financial professional, the truth is that a prospectus will be meaningless for you to even attempt to read. It is as if it is written in a foreign language, and indeed it is a foreign language—it is the language of taxes, investment, and finance. Know your limitations. Have the prospectus explained to you in detail, paragraph by paragraph, by a financial professional whom you trust to have your best interest at heart. And even if you trust the person who is selling you the annuity, you have to recognize that there is an inherent conflict of interest in that relationship. He stands to gain by selling you the annuity. Have another financial professional whom you trust, such as your lawyer or your accountant, explain the annuity prospectus to you. Then you can make your decision.

But don’t throw away that prospectus once you have determined whether or not you are going to buy a particular annuity. Keep it and read it any night you are having trouble sleeping. It will put you to sleep in five minutes.

TRUTH 46

Free looks

"As the old saying goes, what the wise man does in the beginning, fools do in the end."

—Warren Buffet

As I have said throughout this book, there are no free lunches. However, fortunately for purchasers of annuities, state regulators impose laws permitting "free look" periods for anyone purchasing an annuity. These provide annuity buyers with a little time to review the annuity contract before being finally bound to its complicated terms and conditions.

The "free look" period varies from company to company and from state to state, so it is important to look for this feature in your annuity contract when it is first delivered to you. It should be prominently displayed. The minimum "free look" time is 10 days. However, some "free looks" extend as long as 60 days.

The "free look" period varies from company to company and from state to state, so it is important to look for this feature in your annuity contract when it is first delivered to you.

If, after reviewing your annuity, you conclude that the annuity is not an appropriate investment for you, you may terminate the contract with the insurance company and get your money back without having to pay any surrender fee that you would otherwise be liable for in the event of an early termination of your annuity.

Even if you think you understand your annuity, you should take the "free look" to go over the annuity contract in detail—first on your own and then with the insurance salesman who sold you the annuity—to make sure that you fully comprehend all the terms and conditions. You would be wise to also have a lawyer, accountant, or another knowledgeable financial advisor review the annuity on your behalf. The "free look" period is particularly helpful for people who received a hard and quick sell of an annuity without knowing what hit them. Only an unscrupulous salesman would sell an annuity in such fashion, but it happens. The temptation to sell annuities to people even if they are unsuited for them is great due to the high commissions paid for annuity sales.

Annuities are complicated documents. Even if you have been sold one by an ethical insurance agent, this does not mean that it is an investment that complies with your own particular circumstances and wishes. Therefore, it is always important to avail yourself of the "free look" period to better understand the annuity contact, how it affects you, and how it fits into your overall financial plan. Annuities should not be bought in isolation. They should always be a part of a larger, more comprehensive financial plan.

Questions to ask in evaluating an annuity

1. Is the annuity a fixed annuity or variable annuity, and what impact will your choice have on you?
2. Is the annuity an immediate or deferred annuity, and what is the effect on you?
3. How does the cost of this particular annuity compare to similar annuities with other companies?
4. What is the financial strength of the company issuing the annuity?
5. What are the fees involved in the annuity?
6. If it is a deferred annuity, what is the surrender period and what are the surrender fees?
7. How is the interest rate that you will be receiving calculated?
8. What are the income and estate tax ramifications of the annuity?
9. How does the annuity fit into your overall financial plan?
10. What is the death benefit of the annuity, how is it calculated, and what is the cost of this benefit?
11. Is the annuity protected from the claims of creditors in your state?
12. If it is a variable annuity, what are the choices for sub-accounts?
13. What kinds of payouts are available, and what is the most appropriate for you?
14. What will be the income tax effects on you when you start receiving payments?
15. What will be the income and estate tax effects if your children inherit the annuity?
16. Is the annuity for retirement or another long-term goal?

17. Is the salesman urging you to purchase the annuity through an IRA or retirement plan for which it may be unsuited?
18. If it is a variable annuity, are you aware of the risk that your sub-accounts could go down in value?
19. If the annuity offers bonus credits, will the bonus credits be offset by higher fees?
20. Does the annuity offer bells and whistles, such as long-term care benefits, that can be bought more effectively elsewhere?
21. If you are doing a 1035 exchange, are you fully aware of all the costs and the effect of a new surrender period?

Make sure you have the answers to these questions, as well as to any other questions that arise as you go through the annuity contract in detail during the "free look" period.

An annuity is only as good as the company issuing it. You should always check on the rating and strength of the particular company from which you are buying the annuity. You also should only deal with salespeople in whom you have great faith and trust. Positive recommendations from friends and relatives who may have dealt with a particular salesman are always helpful, but just because a friend or relative was comfortable with and trusting of a particular person does not necessarily mean that you should be. Contact your state insurance department and securities regulator to make sure that there are no complaints against the person from whom you are considering buying an annuity.

You also may want to check on the credentials of the particular salesperson looking to sell you an annuity. There are a number of bogus professional designations; however, some in which you can have some faith include the following: Chartered Financial Consultant (ChFC) and Certified Financial Planner (CFP). You can get helpful information from the web sites of the American College, which issues the ChFC at www.amercol.edu; the web site of the Certified Financial Planner Board of Standards at www.cfp.net; and the web site of the Registry of Financial Practitioners at www.fpanet.org.

You also can look for complaints against someone seeking to sell you an annuity at the web site of the Financial Industry Regulatory Authority (FINRA, www.finra.org), formerly the National Association of Securities Dealers).

TRUTH

47

For whom annuities are best

"*An annuity is a very serious business.*"

—Jane Austen

One of the most significant benefits of an annuity is that income taxes on its earnings are deferred until you take money out of the annuity, thereby providing time for your money to grow without being immediately taxed. But is this reason enough to buy an annuity?

No. You can get tax deferrals at less cost to you in fees by paying into a tax-deferred retirement account at work, like a 401(k). In fact, your employer may even match your contribution to your 401(k), thereby giving you free money, which beats added fees any day and also provides a tremendous incentive to invest in your 401(k) at work before you ever consider buying an annuity. In addition, the money that you invest in your 401(k) is money that is pretax. That means that you do not have to pay income taxes on the money before you put it to work for you in your 401(k). So, maximize your 401(k) before buying an annuity.

Maximize your 401(k) before buying an annuity.

Even if you have a 401(k) at work, you may also wish to put your money into a traditional IRA that, if you qualify, will provide you with a tax deduction now in addition to income tax deferral. An annuity can provide you with tax deferral, but it can't provide you with an income tax deduction. So, maximize your contribution to a traditional IRA before you consider buying an annuity.

Or maybe you want to consider putting your money into a Roth IRA that won't provide you with an income tax deduction, but even better than tax deferral, the money that accumulates in your Roth IRA does so totally tax-free, which is a benefit that no annuity can promise.

As with traditional IRAs and other retirement accounts, there are significant penalties if you need to take money out of an annuity before you reach the magic age of 59 ½. If you are concerned that you may need access to the money that you are investing in an annuity, you may want to consider as an alternative, investing in index mutual funds that have far fewer fees than are found in annuities and contain no penalties for withdrawal of your money before you reach 59 ½.

Speaking of fees. Annuity fees can dramatically reduce the value of your investment, particularly if you need to take money out of your annuity before you reach the age of 59 ½ and have not owned your annuity long enough to eliminate costly surrender fees. Frankly, unless you expect to hold your annuity for at least fifteen years, you are better off just buying index mutual funds.

Don't forget that you may have deferred income taxes with an annuity, but you have not eliminated them. So if you think you are not going to be in a much lower income tax bracket when you start to take money out of your annuity, an annuity may not be for you. And because as the money comes out of your annuity, your earnings are taxed at higher ordinary income tax rates instead of the lower capital gains rates that you would be taxed at if you had invested in mutual funds.

If you wish to leave money to your heirs through your annuity, it is also important to remember that they will be paying income tax at ordinary income tax rates on the earnings of the annuity, rather than paying capital gains income tax rates on property with a stepped-up basis. This is what they would be doing had you invested in a mutual fund that they inherited. With a stepped-up basis, you might have had a mutual fund that increased in value by 100% during your lifetime, but would pass at your death to your heirs at the value that it was at the time of your death, so that if they sell the mutual fund at that time, they would have absolutely no income tax liability at all. If you are thinking of an annuity as an investment to leave to your heirs, you may want to consider plain old life insurance. Held in an irrevocable life insurance trust, the life insurance proceeds can be paid to multiple generations tax-free.

All of this makes annuities look like not such a good investment unless you have maxed out your other tax-advantaged investments, expect to leave the money in the annuity alone to grow without touching it for fifteen years or more, are in a higher income tax bracket today than you expect to be when you retire, are not concerned that you may need to get at the money

All of this makes annuities look like not such a good investment unless you have maxed out your other tax-advantaged investments.

> Yet there are people for whom annuities make a lot of sense.

before you reach the age of 59 ½, and are not concerned about the adverse income tax and estate tax aspects of annuities. And all of this may be true, yet there are people for whom annuities make a lot of sense.

An *immediate annuity* that you purchase at retirement that guarantees you a steady income for the rest of your life and that of your spouse can offer some real peace of mind for people who are afraid (perhaps justifiably) of the stock market, particularly in the short run. A *fixed immediate annuity* will pay you a specific amount each month based on your age and the amount of money you invest with the insurance company; however, although the amount that you receive each month is guaranteed, it is definitely not guaranteed to keep up with inflation. An *immediate variable annuity* with mutual fund sub-accounts presents you with a greater opportunity to keep up with inflation, although it also brings significantly greater fees than those you pay in a fixed immediate annuity.

Shop around. Although fees ultimately present the biggest downside to annuities, not all annuities are created equally. There are a number of companies, such as TIAA-CREF, Vanguard, and Fidelity, that offer annuities with far lower fees than you may find at other companies. Annuity sales are a competitive business. Do your homework and compare costs to find what annuity may work best for you.

One little noted, but valuable, advantage to having annuities as a part of your retirement investment portfolio is that by having some of your retirement eggs in the secure basket of a low-cost fixed immediate annuity, you are in a better position to be a bit more aggressive with the rest of your portfolio, confident that your investments are diversified by having a portion of your money in conservative, guaranteed annuities.

TRUTH 48

Steve's annuity rules, part one

"I always pass on good advice. It is the thing to do with it. It is never of any use to oneself."

—Oscar Wilde

You can't play the game unless you know the rules. Here are some of my rules about annuities that you should know.

Rule one—In any investment, it is not what you make that counts—it is what you keep. Fees are a critical element in evaluating the appropriateness of any investment. Annuities come fraught with many fees, some of which are not obvious. Make sure you know what the fees are and how they affect the value of your investment before you invest in an annuity (or anything else, for that matter). Remember that not all annuities are the same when it comes to fees. There are some good annuities with low fees out there. You just have to look for them.

In any investment, it is not what you make that counts—it is what you keep. Fees are a critical element in evaluating the appropriateness of any investment.

Rule two—In any investment, it is not what you make that counts—it is what you keep. I know, this is the same as Rule One, but it is so important that it qualifies for two rules.

Rule three—The longer you are able to keep your money in a deferred annuity without needing the money, the greater will be your return.

Rule four—Do not consider investing in an annuity until you have invested all you can in IRAs and 401(k)s available to you.

Rule five—Tax deferral is good. Paying no taxes is better. A Roth IRA always beats an annuity. If you qualify, get a Roth IRA before you get an annuity.

Rule six—No investment is foolproof. The power of fools is extraordinary. It is possible to lose money in an equity indexed annuity if you have to cash in the annuity during a time when the stock market is down and you are subject to a substantial surrender fee. Always consider equity indexed annuities as a long-term investment.

Rule seven—Never invest money in an annuity that you may possibly need before you reach the age of 59 ½.

Rule eight—Beware of Greeks bearing gifts. All right, it is a little late for this advice for the residents of the ancient city of Troy, who failed to heed this warning when they took the Trojan horse into their city. They thought that after ten years of war, the Greeks had given up, gone home and left the Trojan horse as a lovely parting gift. It was not. It was loaded with Greek soldiers who destroyed Troy. Likewise, beware of annuity salespeople who try to talk you into a 1035 annuity exchange. The 1035 annuity exchange may, in fact, be a good deal for you, or it may be just a good deal for the salesperson and a lousy deal for you. Be an educated consumer. Check out the fees and new surrender charges. And if your annuity salesperson's name is Odysseus, don't accept any gifts. Trust me.

Rule nine—Investing in an annuity in your IRA does not make sense, but in some limited circumstances, investing in an annuity through your 401(k) may make sense.

Rule ten—Annuities are not a good investment to leave to your heirs.

Rule eleven—Owning mutual funds in a variable annuity is ultimately more expensive than owning mutual funds outside of a variable annuity, but that is not the whole story. For some people who are particularly active traders, variable annuities may meet their needs better than merely owning mutual funds.

Rule twelve—Annuities are an effective way for elderly married couples to legally shelter assets in order to qualify one of them for long-term nursing home care through Medicaid. That being said, using annuities as a part of Medicaid planning is very complicated. There are specific state and federal rules that pertain to the provisions that must be contained in an annuity to be used for this purpose. Using annuities to assist in Medicaid eligibility should only be done in conjunction with planning prepared by an elder law attorney.

Rule thirteen—Annuities are not a great investment for children, but a Roth IRA for a child may offer tremendous value.

Rule fourteen—Annuity death benefits aren't that much of a benefit.

Rule fifteen—If an annuity salesperson tells you that you do not pay a commission on the purchase of an annuity from him, he is misleading you. You may not pay the commission directly, but you pay it through higher annuity fees that you pay each year.

Rule sixteen—You should not buy a deferred variable annuity unless you are confident that you will not need the money for at least ten and preferably fifteen years.

Rule seventeen—Not all annuities are created equal. There is a great deal of variation in the amount of fees that are charged by various issuers of annuities. Remember Rule One. Investigate what companies will offer you the benefits you need at the least amount of cost before you buy an annuity.

Rule eighteen—Your annuity is only as good as the company from which you buy it. Always research the strength of the company and its rating with the major rating services before buying an annuity.

TRUTH 49

Steve's annuity rules, part two

"Many receive advice, only the wise profit from it."

—Publilius Syrus

Personal finances are complicated. However, knowing certain basic rules can go a long way toward simplifying the process and making your decisions easier. Here are more rules to help you understand some basic truths about annuities.

Rule nineteen—Consider a lifetime payout annuity option if your family is one with longevity.

Rule twenty—Every added feature of an annuity comes at a price. Make sure you understand the cost to you of any "bells and whistles" contained in an annuity that you may be considering.

Every added feature of an annuity comes at a price. Make sure you understand the cost to you of any "bells and whistles" contained in an annuity that you may be considering.

Rule twenty-one—Free bonus credits in annuities are not free.

Rule twenty-two—In an equity indexed annuity, not only is the particular index used important, but also important is the method used to determine changes in the index and when they will benefit you.

Rule twenty-three—A charitable gift annuity may be a way to guarantee an income stream to you in retirement, get a current tax deduction, and benefit a worthy charity, but you still must do your homework.

Rule twenty-four—If you buy a fixed annuity, look for the longest guaranteed interest rate period you can get and make sure that the surrender period does not last longer than the interest rate guarantee period. This way, if you choose to get out of the annuity when your interest rate guarantee is up, you don't have to pay a surrender fee.

Rule twenty-five—Annuities work best if you expect to be in a lower tax bracket when you retire.

Rule twenty-six—Avoid inflation-protected annuities. The protection you get is not worth the cost. Instead consider splitting your money between a fixed immediate annuity and an index mutual fund.

Consider splitting your money between a fixed immediate annuity and an index mutual fund.

Rule twenty-seven—Owning a low-cost immediate annuity at retirement may put you into a better position to be more aggressive with the rest of your investment portfolio.

Rule twenty-eight—You can change the mixture and proportions of the mutual fund sub-accounts in your variable annuity without incurring any income taxes.

Rule twenty-nine—Equity indexed annuities do not guarantee that you will benefit by all increases in the stock index you choose.

Rule thirty—If you do not expect to purchase an annuity until you are in your 70s, a traditional deferred annuity will be a better deal for you than the new longevity insurance annuity.

Rule thirty-one—Shorter surrender period annuities generally have higher fees that can substantially negate the value of the shorter surrender period.

Rule thirty-two—Laddering fixed immediate annuities can be an effective strategy to take advantage of rising interest rates and obtain a higher monthly annuity payout.

Rule thirty-three—Life should have more "free looks." When you buy an annuity, you have a "free look" period to review your annuity and re-evaluate its appropriateness for you. Take advantage of your "free look."

Rule thirty-four—The split annuity strategy can be a safe way to stay current with interest rate fluctuations and make retirement investment dollars work longer for you.

Rule thirty-five—In many circumstances, taking a lifetime only payout from your annuity and providing for your spouse's needs if you should predecease her through life insurance is a better choice than a joint life and survivor payout.

Rule thirty-six—When necessary, purchasing an immediate annuity with money obtained through a reverse mortgage can be an effective reverse mortgage strategy.

Rule thirty-seven—In any investment, it is not what you make that is important—it is what you keep. I know. I know. This is the third time I have said this rule, but there is a reason for doing this. This is the most important rule when it comes to any investment, but particularly annuities, which may come with a wide array of fees that can eat into your profits. Look for low-cost annuities with few fees. With these, your investment works better for you.

TRUTH

50

Where to go for information

"Information is the seed for an idea, and only grows when it's watered."

—Heinz V. Bergen

It is easy to find places to go to for information about annuities. Unfortunately, much of this information is skewed by the fact that it is provided by people who are seeking to sell you an annuity. However, there are a number of places you can go to for information about annuities that you can rely on. Here are some of them.

The Securities and Exchange Commission's web site is full of good information about annuities:

- www.sec.gov/investor/seniors/seniorscarepackage.htm
- www.sec.gov/investor/pubs/equityidxannuity.htm
- www.sec.gov/investor/pubs/varaquestions.htm

The Financial Industry Regulatory Authority also has a lot of good information about annuities. Type in the word "annuities" in the search box for a number of good articles on annuities:

- www.finra.org

ImmediateAnnuities.com is a web site where you can get online quotes and comparisons of various fixed annuities. It is easy to use:

- www.immediateannuities.com

The Healthcare and Elder Law Programs Corporation (HELP) is a non-profit education and counseling center that sponsors a web site with much information about annuities:

- www.annuitytruth.org

You can't have too much information when you are comparing and evaluating specific annuities. Annuity FYI is a good web site for comparing various types of annuities and the riders that they have. It is well organized and is a great starting point for narrowing your search for a particular annuity, whether it is a variable annuity or a fixed annuity:

- www.annuityfyi.com

Annuities-Central.com is another online source of information about annuities, as well as a source from which you can obtain prices for purchasing an annuity. As with any web site that sells annuities, it is important to remember that their primary goal is to sell you an annuity. Always be cognizant of this fact when considering the information about annuities provided on this or any other web site that sells you anything:

- www.annuities-central.com

The Variable Annuity Research and Data Service (VARDS) provides valuable information and analysis on investment portfolios used in variable annuities. This information can help you determine the proper investment mix of sub-accounts in a variable annuity for you. Morningstar, one of the best sources of independent investment information, operates VARDS:

- www.vards.com

In addition to these sites, you can also get information from any of the myriad of insurance companies, brokerage houses, and mutual fund companies that sell annuities. Many of these companies have useful online calculators for your use as well. Some examples of insurance companies, mutual fund companies, and brokerage companies that have useful web sites are the following:

- Columbus Life Insurance Company—www.columbuslife.com
- Vanguard—www.vanguard.com
- Charles Schwab—www.schwab.com
- TIAA-CREF—www.tiaa-cref

The mutual fund companies, such as Vanguard, and the discount brokers, such as Schwab, sell very competitively priced annuities. TIAA-CREF, which limits its sales to those in the academic and medical professions, also sells annuities with fewer fees. As always, when you are gathering information from a source that also sells annuities, you have to be cognizant of the fact that they stand to gain from selling you an annuity, and there will be a bias to their information. However, this is not a bad thing. It is just something to be aware of when you evaluate the information presented. Be a savvy consumer when you gather information.

Your annuity is only as good as the person who sells it to you. In order to evaluate the salesperson, you should check out him or her at the web site of the Financial Industry Regulatory Authority (FINRA):

- www.finra.org

If you want to check the qualifications of the person selling you an annuity, you also can go to the following web sites:

- www.amercol.edu, which is the web site of the American College (which issues the ChFC).
- www.cfp.net, which is the web site of the Certified Financial Planner Board of Standards.
- www.fpa.net, which is the web site of the Registry of Financial Practitioners.

An annuity is a long-term commitment that is guaranteed by the insurance company issuing the annuity. It is imperative that you consider the financial strength of the particular company from which you are considering buying an annuity. You can find ratings of these companies through the following web sites:

- www.ambest.com for AM Best
- www.standardandandpoors.com for Standard & Poor's
- www.moodys.com for Moody's
- www.weissratings.com for Weiss

It is easy to find places to go to for information about annuities. Unfortunately, much of this information is skewed by the fact that it is provided by people who are seeking to sell you an annuity.

If you are considering purchasing a charitable gift annuity, you can find financial information on the charity issuing the annuity at the web site of the American Institute of Philanthropy:

- www.charitywatch.org

If you are considering using an annuity in combination with a reverse mortgage, you can obtain some helpful information at the following web sites:

- www.reversemortgage.org, which is the web site of the National Reverse Mortgage Lender's Association.
- www.rmaarp.com, which is a part of the AARP web site that contains a helpful interactive calculator.

About the Author

Steve Weisman is Senior Lecturer at Bentley College in the department of Law, Tax, and Financial Planning. He has also taught courses on financial planning at the University of Massachusetts, Curry College, and Boston University. He is a host on the nationally syndicated radio show *A Touch of Grey*, heard on more than 50 stations, including NYC's legendary WABC and KRLA Los Angeles. A member of the National Association of Elder Law Attorneys, Weisman is legal editor and columnist for *Talkers Magazine* and writes for publications ranging from *The Boston Globe* to *US Air*. His books include *Boomer or Bust* and *The Truth About Avoiding Scams*. Weisman has earned a Certificate of Merit for legal journalism from the American Bar Association.